Southern COOKING

Publications International, Ltd.
Favorite Brand Name Recipes at www.fbnr.com

Pictured on the front cover: Southern Buttermilk Fried Chicken *(page 82)*.

Pictured on the back cover *(top to bottom):* Hoppin' John Soup *(page 60),* Savory Chicken and Biscuits *(page 110)* and Crunch Peach Cobbler *(page180)*.

Photography on the front cover by Chris Cassidy Photography, Inc.

Illustrations by Joel Spector.

ISBN: 1-4127-2171-7

Library of Congress Control Number: 2005920745

Manufactured in China.

8 7 6 5 4 3 2 1

Microwave Cooking: Microwave ovens vary in wattage. Use the cooking times as guidelines and check for doneness before adding more time.

Preparation/Cooking Times: Preparation times are based on the approximate amount of time required to assemble the recipe before cooking, baking, chilling or serving. These times include preparation steps such as measuring, chopping and mixing. The fact that some preparations and cooking can be done simultaneously is taken into account. Preparation of optional ingredients and serving suggestions is not included.

Contents

VERANDA

Party Foods

Honey Roasted Ham Biscuits

1 (10-ounce) can refrigerated buttermilk biscuits
2 cups (12 ounces) diced CURE 81® ham
½ cup honey mustard
¼ cup finely chopped honey roasted peanuts, divided

Heat oven to 400°F. Separate biscuits. Place in muffin pans, pressing gently into bottom and up sides of pan. In bowl, combine ham, honey mustard and 2 tablespoons peanuts. Spoon ham mixture evenly into biscuit cups. Sprinkle with remaining 2 tablespoons peanuts. Bake 15 to 17 minutes.

Makes 10 servings

Honey Roasted Ham Biscuits

Crab Canapés

⅔ cup cream cheese, softened
2 teaspoons lemon juice
1 teaspoon hot pepper sauce
1 package (8 ounces) imitation crabmeat or lobster, flaked
⅓ cup chopped red bell pepper
2 green onions with tops, sliced (about ¼ cup)
64 cucumber slices (about 2½ medium cucumbers cut into
⅜-inch-thick slices) or melba toast rounds
Fresh parsley, for garnish (optional)

1. Combine cream cheese, lemon juice and hot pepper sauce in medium bowl; mix well. Stir in crabmeat, bell pepper and green onions; cover. Chill until ready to serve.

2. When ready to serve, spoon 1½ teaspoons crabmeat mixture onto each cucumber slice. Place on serving plate; garnish with parsley, if desired.

Makes 16 servings

To allow the flavors to blend, chill the crab mixture at least 1 hour before spreading onto the cucumbers. Or, assemble canapés about 1 hour before serving and arrange on a serving plate. Cover tightly with plastic wrap and refrigerate until ready to serve.

Crab Canapés

Cheese Straws

½ cup (1 stick) butter, softened
⅛ teaspoon salt
   Dash ground red pepper
1 pound sharp Cheddar cheese, shredded, at room temperature
2 cups self-rising flour

Heat oven to 350°F. In mixer bowl, beat butter, salt and pepper until creamy. Add cheese; mix well. Gradually add flour, mixing until dough begins to form a ball. Form dough into ball with hands. Fit cookie press with small star plate; fill with dough according to manufacturer's directions. Press dough onto cookie sheets in 3-inch-long strips (or desired shapes). Bake 12 minutes, just until lightly browned. Cool completely on wire rack. Store tightly covered.   ***Makes about 10 dozen straws***

Favorite recipe from **Southeast United Dairy Industry Association, Inc.**

Hot Pepper Cranberry Jelly Appetizer

½ cup canned whole cranberry sauce
¼ cup apricot fruit spread
1 teaspoon sugar
1 teaspoon cider vinegar
½ teaspoon dried red pepper flakes
½ teaspoon grated fresh ginger
   Crackers and cheeses

1. Combine cranberry sauce, fruit spread, sugar, vinegar and pepper flakes in small saucepan. Cook over medium heat until sugar has dissolved; do not boil. Transfer to bowl to cool completely. Stir in ginger.

2. To serve, top crackers with cheese and a dollop of cranberry-apricot mixture.   ***Makes 16 appetizer servings***

Cheese Straws

Iced Tea

2½ tablespoons Time-Saver Sugar Syrup (recipe follows)
1 cup double-strength hot tea
Crushed ice

Add Time-Saver Sugar Syrup to tea; stir well. Fill 2 glasses with crushed ice; pour tea mixture over ice. Serve cold. *Makes 2 servings*

NOTE: To prepare double-strength tea, bring 1 cup water to a boil; add 2 tea bags. Steep 3 to 5 minutes. Discard tea bags.

Favorite recipe from **The Sugar Association, Inc.**

Time-Saver Sugar Syrup

1 cup water
2 cups sugar

Combine water and sugar in medium saucepan. Cook and stir over medium heat until sugar dissolves. Cool to room temperature; strain through sieve. Refrigerate until chilled. *Makes about 2 cups syrup*

Favorite recipe from **The Sugar Association, Inc.**

Shrimp Spread

½ **pound medium shrimp, peeled and deveined, reserving shells**
1 **cup water**
½ **teaspoon onion powder**
½ **teaspoon garlic salt**
1 **package (8 ounces) cream cheese, softened**
¼ **cup (½ stick) butter, softened**
2 **tablespoons mayonnaise**
2 **tablespoons cocktail sauce**
1 **tablespoon lemon juice**
1 **tablespoon chopped fresh parsley**
    Assorted crackers or raw vegetables

1. Place reserved shrimp shells, water, onion powder and garlic salt in medium saucepan. Bring to a simmer over medium heat; simmer 5 minutes. Remove shells and discard. Add shrimp; simmer 1 minute or until shrimp turn pink and opaque. Remove shrimp to cutting board; let cool. Continue cooking shrimp liquid; reduce to about 3 tablespoons.

2. Blend cream cheese, butter, mayonnaise, cocktail sauce and lemon juice in large bowl until smooth. Stir in 1 tablespoon reduced cooking liquid. Discard remaining liquid.

3. Finely chop shrimp. Fold shrimp and parsley into cheese mixture.

4. Pack spread into decorative serving crock or mold lined with plastic wrap. Cover; refrigerate overnight. Serve spread in crock or invert mold onto serving platter. Remove plastic wrap. Serve with assorted crackers.

Makes 2½ to 3 cups

Quick Pimiento Cheese Snacks

2 ounces cream cheese, softened
½ cup (2 ounces) shredded Cheddar cheese
1 jar (2 ounces) diced pimientos, drained
2 tablespoons finely chopped pecans
½ teaspoon hot pepper sauce
24 (¼-inch-thick) French bread slices or party bread slices

1. Preheat broiler.

2. Combine cream cheese and Cheddar cheese in small bowl; mix well. Stir in pimientos, pecans and hot pepper sauce.

3. Place bread slices on broiler pan or nonstick baking sheet. Broil 4 inches from heat 1 to 2 minutes or until lightly toasted on both sides.

4. Spread cheese mixture evenly onto bread slices. Broil 1 to 2 minutes or until cheese mixture is hot and bubbly. Transfer to serving plate.

Makes 24 servings

Hot Spiced Tea

4 cups freshly brewed tea
¼ cup honey
4 cinnamon sticks
4 whole cloves
4 lemon or orange slices (optional)

Combine tea, honey, cinnamon sticks and cloves in large saucepan; simmer 5 minutes. Serve hot. Garnish with lemon slices, if desired.

Makes 4 cups

Favorite recipe from **National Honey Board**

Quick Pimiento Cheese Snacks

Louisiana Crab Dip with Crudités

1 package (8 ounces) cream cheese, softened
½ cup sour cream
3 tablespoons horseradish
2 tablespoons chopped fresh parsley
1 tablespoon coarse ground mustard
2 teaspoons TABASCO® brand Pepper Sauce
1 cup lump crabmeat
1 bunch baby carrots
1 bunch celery, cut into sticks
1 bunch asparagus spears, blanched
2 bunches endive
2 red or green bell peppers, cored and cut into strips

Blend cream cheese, sour cream, horseradish, parsley, mustard and TABASCO® Sauce in medium bowl until well mixed. Stir in crabmeat.

Arrange carrots, celery, asparagus, endive and peppers on large platter. Serve with dip. *Makes about 2 cups dip*

Louisiana Crab Dip with Crudités

Sausage Pinwheels

2 cups biscuit mix
½ cup milk
¼ cup butter or margarine, melted
1 pound BOB EVANS® Original Recipe Roll Sausage

Combine biscuit mix, milk and butter in large bowl until blended. Refrigerate 30 minutes. Divide dough into two portions. Roll out one portion on floured surface to ⅛-inch-thick rectangle, about 10×7 inches. Spread with half the sausage. Roll lengthwise into long roll. Repeat with remaining dough and sausage. Place rolls in freezer until firm enough to cut easily. Preheat oven to 400°F. Cut rolls into thin slices. Place on baking sheets. Bake 15 minutes or until golden brown. Serve hot. Refrigerate leftovers.

Makes 48 pinwheels

Be prepared for a last minute party.
Double this recipe. Then, refreeze some of the
pinwheels after slicing. When ready to serve,
thaw the slices in the refrigerator and bake.

Sausage Pinwheels

Citrus Mint Tea Cooler

1 cup boiling water
3 tea bags
2 tablespoons chopped fresh mint leaves
⅓ cup sugar or to taste
2 cups cold water
  Juice of 3 SUNKIST® lemons (½ cup)
  Juice of 1 SUNKIST® grapefruit
  Ice cubes

In large pitcher, pour boiling water over tea bags and mint leaves. Cover and steep 5 minutes; strain. Stir in sugar. Add cold water, lemon and grapefruit juices. Serve over ice. Garnish with lemon cartwheel slices and fresh mint leaves, if desired.   *Makes 4 (8-ounce) servings*

Peppered Pecans

3 tablespoons butter or margarine
3 cloves garlic, minced
1½ teaspoons TABASCO® brand Pepper Sauce
½ teaspoon salt
3 cups pecan halves

Preheat oven to 250°F. Melt butter in small skillet. Add garlic, TABASCO® Sauce and salt; cook 1 minute. Toss pecans with butter mixture; spread in single layer on baking sheet. Bake 1 hour or until pecans are crisp, stirring occasionally.   *Makes 3 cups pecans*

Sausage Cheese Puffs

1 pound BOB EVANS® Original Recipe Roll Sausage
2½ cups (10 ounces) shredded sharp Cheddar cheese
2 cups biscuit mix
½ cup water
1 teaspoon baking powder

Preheat oven to 350°F. Combine ingredients in large bowl until blended. Shape into 1-inch balls. Place on lightly greased baking sheets. Bake about 25 minutes or until golden brown. Serve hot. Refrigerate leftovers.

Makes about 60 appetizers

Kahlúa® & Eggnog

1 quart dairy eggnog
¾ cup KAHLÚA® Liqueur
Whipped cream
Ground nutmeg

Combine eggnog and Kahlúa® in 1½-quart pitcher. Pour into punch cups. Top with whipped cream. Sprinkle with nutmeg.

Makes about 8 servings

Baltimore Crab Cakes

16 ounces lump crabmeat, picked over and flaked
1 cup saltine cracker crumbs, divided
2 eggs, lightly beaten
¼ cup chopped green onions
¼ cup minced fresh parsley
¼ cup mayonnaise
2 tablespoons fresh lemon juice
1 teaspoon green pepper sauce
¼ teaspoon salt
   Black pepper
¼ cup vegetable oil
2 tablespoons butter
   Lemon wedges

1. Combine crab, ¼ cup cracker crumbs, eggs, green onions, parsley, mayonnaise, lemon juice, pepper sauce, salt and pepper to taste in medium bowl; mix well. Shape mixture into 12 cakes, using ¼ cup crab mixture for each.

2. Place remaining ¾ cup cracker crumbs in shallow bowl. Coat crab cakes with crumb mixture, lightly pressing crumbs into cakes. Place cakes on plate; cover and refrigerate 30 minutes to 1 hour.

3. Heat oil and butter in large skillet over medium heat until butter is melted. Cook crab cakes 3 to 4 minutes until golden brown on bottoms. Turn and cook 3 minutes until golden brown and internal temperature reaches 170°F. Serve immediately with lemon wedges.

Makes 12 servings

Baltimore Crab Cakes

Pineapple-Almond Cheese Spread

2 cans (8 ounces each) DOLE® Crushed Pineapple
1 package (8 ounces) cream cheese, softened
4 cups (16 ounces) shredded sharp Cheddar cheese
½ cup mayonnaise
1 tablespoon soy sauce
1 cup chopped almonds, toasted
½ cup finely chopped DOLE® Green Bell Pepper
¼ cup minced green onions or chives
  DOLE® Celery stalks or assorted breads

• Drain crushed pineapple. In large bowl, beat cream cheese until smooth; beat in Cheddar cheese, mayonnaise and soy sauce until smooth. Stir in crushed pineapple, almonds, green pepper and onions. Refrigerate, covered. Use to stuff celery stalks or serve as spread with assorted breads. Serve at room temperature. *Makes 4 cups*

Cheese spreads are fabulous party foods because they are easy to prepare and serve. They can be made ahead of time, refrigerated and served at the last minute with vegetables or crispy crackers. For a fancy presentation, pack the spread in molds lined with plastic wrap. Invert the molds on decorative serving plates. Remove the plastic wrap and serve.

Mini Sausage Quiches

½ **cup butter or margarine, softened**
3 **ounces cream cheese, softened**
1 **cup all-purpose flour**
½ **pound BOB EVANS® Italian Roll Sausage**
1 **cup (4 ounces) shredded Swiss cheese**
1 **tablespoon snipped fresh chives**
2 **eggs**
1 **cup half-and-half**
¼ **teaspoon salt**
  Dash cayenne pepper

Beat butter and cream cheese in medium bowl until creamy. Blend in flour; refrigerate 1 hour. Roll into 24 (1-inch) balls; press each into ungreased mini-muffin cup to form pastry shell. Preheat oven to 375°F. To prepare filling, crumble sausage into small skillet. Cook over medium heat until browned, stirring occasionally. Drain off any drippings. Sprinkle evenly into pastry shells in muffin cups; sprinkle with Swiss cheese and chives. Whisk eggs, half-and-half, salt and cayenne until blended; pour into pastry shells. Bake 20 to 30 minutes or until set. Remove from pans. Serve hot. Refrigerate leftovers. *Makes 24 appetizers*

TIP: Use 12 standard 2½-inch muffin cups to make larger individual quiches. Serve for breakfast.

Devilish Crab Puffs

Swiss Puffs (page 26)
2 cups crabmeat, cleaned
¼ cup chopped fresh parsley
¼ cup mayonnaise
2 tablespoons finely minced onion
2 teaspoons white wine
1 teaspoon Worcestershire sauce
1 teaspoon dry mustard
1 teaspoon lemon juice
¼ teaspoon white pepper

1. Prepare Swiss Puffs; set aside.

2. To make filling, place crabmeat in medium bowl. Add parsley, mayonnaise, onion, wine, Worcestershire sauce, mustard, lemon juice and pepper. Stir gently to blend.

3. Preheat oven to 375°F. Fill Swiss Puffs with crab filling.

4. Place filled appetizers on ungreased baking sheet; bake 10 minutes or until heated through.   *Makes about 40 appetizers*

Devilish Crab Puffs

Swiss Puffs

½ cup milk
½ cup water
¼ cup (½ stick) butter
¼ teaspoon salt
  Pinch ground nutmeg
  Pinch white pepper
1 cup all-purpose flour
4 eggs, at room temperature
1 cup shredded Swiss cheese, divided

1. Preheat oven to 400°F. Grease 2 large baking sheets.

2. Heat milk, water, butter, salt, nutmeg and pepper in 3-quart saucepan over medium-high heat until mixture boils. Remove pan from heat; add flour all at once, mixing until smooth. Cook over medium-low heat, stirring constantly, until mixture leaves side of pan clean and forms a ball. Remove pan from heat.

3. Add eggs, 1 at a time, beating until smooth and shiny after each addition. Continue beating until mixture loses its gloss. Stir in ¾ cup cheese.

4. Drop rounded teaspoonfuls of batter 1 inch apart onto prepared baking sheets. Sprinkle with remaining ¼ cup cheese.

5. Bake 30 to 35 minutes or until puffs are golden brown. Cool completely on wire racks.

6. Before filling, cut tops off puffs; scoop out and discard moist dough in centers.   *Makes about 4 dozen*

Real Old-Fashioned Lemonade

Juice of 6 SUNKIST® lemons (1 cup)
¾ cup sugar, or to taste
4 cups cold water
1 SUNKIST® lemon, cut into cartwheel slices
Ice cubes

In large pitcher, combine lemon juice and sugar; stir to dissolve sugar. Add remaining ingredients; blend well. *Makes about 6 cups*

PINK LEMONADE: Add a few drops of red food coloring or grenadine syrup.

HONEYED LEMONADE: Substitute honey to taste for the sugar.

Spicy Marinated Shrimp

1 green onion, finely chopped
2 tablespoons olive oil
2 tablespoons fresh lemon juice
2 tablespoons prepared horseradish
2 tablespoons ketchup
1 tablespoon finely chopped chives
1 teaspoon TABASCO® brand Pepper Sauce
1 teaspoon Dijon mustard
1 clove garlic, minced
   Salt to taste
2 pounds medium shrimp, cooked, peeled and deveined

Combine all ingredients except shrimp in large bowl. Add shrimp and toss to coat. Cover and refrigerate 4 to 6 hours or overnight. Transfer shrimp mixture to serving bowl and serve with toothpicks.   *Makes 30 to 40 shrimp*

Spicy Marinated Shrimp

Barbecued Peanuts

¼ cup barbecue sauce
2 tablespoons butter, melted
¾ teaspoon garlic salt
⅛ teaspoon ground red pepper*
1 jar (16 ounces) dry roasted lightly salted peanuts

*For Spicy Barbecued Peanuts, increase ground red pepper to ¼ teaspoon.

1. Preheat oven to 325°F. Grease 13×9-inch baking pan. Set aside.

2. Whisk barbecue sauce, melted butter, garlic salt and pepper in medium bowl with wire whisk until well blended. Add peanuts; toss until evenly coated.

3. Spread peanuts in single layer in prepared pan.

4. Bake 20 to 22 minutes or until peanuts are glazed, stirring occasionally. Cool completely in pan on wire rack, stirring occasionally to prevent peanuts from sticking together.

5. Spoon into clean, dry decorative tin; cover. Store tightly covered at room temperature up to 2 weeks.   *Makes about 4 cups*

Peanuts can be successfully stored for a long time. Unopened vacuum-packed shelled peanuts can be stored at room temperature for up to 1 year. Once opened, peanuts should be refrigerated in an airtight container and used within 3 months.

Deviled Shrimp

Devil Sauce (recipe follows)
2 eggs, lightly beaten
¼ teaspoon salt
¼ teaspoon TABASCO® brand Pepper Sauce
1 quart vegetable oil
1 pound raw shrimp, peeled and cleaned
1 cup dry bread crumbs

Prepare Devil Sauce; set aside. Stir together eggs, salt and TABASCO® Sauce in shallow dish until well blended. Pour oil into heavy 3-quart saucepan or deep-fat fryer, filling no more than ⅓ full. Heat oil over medium heat to 375°F. Dip shrimp into egg mixture, then into bread crumbs; shake off excess. Carefully add shrimp to oil, a few at a time. Cook 1 to 2 minutes or until golden. Drain on paper towels. Just before serving, drizzle Devil Sauce over shrimp. *Makes 6 appetizer servings*

Devil Sauce

2 tablespoons butter or margarine
1 small onion, finely chopped
1 clove garlic, minced
1½ teaspoons dry mustard
½ cup beef consommé
2 tablespoons Worcestershire sauce
2 tablespoons dry white wine
¼ teaspoon TABASCO® brand Pepper Sauce
¼ cup lemon juice

Melt butter in 1-quart saucepan over medium heat; add onion and garlic. Stirring frequently, cook 3 minutes or until tender. Blend in mustard. Gradually stir in consommé, Worcestershire sauce, wine and TABASCO® Sauce until well blended. Bring to a boil and simmer 5 minutes. Stir in lemon juice. Serve warm over shrimp or use as a dip. *Makes about 1¼ cups*

Festive Crab Toasts

12 ounces crabmeat, flaked
1 can (10¾ ounces) condensed cream of celery soup, undiluted
¼ cup chopped celery
¼ cup sliced green onions
1 tablespoon lemon juice
⅛ teaspoon grated lemon peel
1 (8-ounce) French bread baguette
⅓ cup grated Parmesan cheese
    Paprika

1. Combine crabmeat, soup, celery, onions, lemon juice and lemon peel in medium bowl; mix well. Cut baguette diagonally into ½-inch slices; arrange slices on 2 ungreased baking sheets. Broil 5 inches from heat 2 minutes or until toasted, turning once.

2. Spread 1 tablespoon crab mixture onto each baguette slice. Top with Parmesan cheese; sprinkle with paprika. Broil 5 inches from heat 2 minutes or until lightly browned. **Makes about 30 appetizers**

Festive Crab Toasts

SOUTHERN
Breads

Savory Corn Cakes

2 cups all-purpose flour
1 teaspoon baking powder
½ teaspoon salt
2 cups frozen corn, thawed
1 cup (4 ounces) shredded smoked Cheddar cheese
1 cup milk
2 egg whites, beaten
1 whole egg, beaten
4 green onions, finely chopped
2 cloves garlic, minced
1 tablespoon chili powder
  Prepared salsa (optional)

1. Combine flour, baking powder and salt in large bowl. Add corn, cheese, milk, egg whites, egg, green onions, garlic and chili powder; stir until well blended.

2. Spray large nonstick skillet with nonstick cooking spray; heat over medium-high heat.

3. Drop batter by ¼ cupfuls into skillet. Cook 3 minutes per side or until golden brown. Serve with salsa, if desired.   ***Makes 12 cakes***

Savory Corn Cakes

Bourbon Street Beignet Puffs

CRISCO® Shortening for deep frying
1 cup water
½ cup butter
¼ teaspoon salt
1 cup all-purpose flour
1 tablespoon plus 1½ teaspoons granulated sugar
4 eggs (at room temperature)
1½ teaspoons vanilla
Confectioners' sugar

Heat 2 or 3 inches CRISCO® Shortening to 365°F in deep fryer or deep saucepan.

In a separate saucepan, combine water, butter and salt. Bring to a boil.

Add flour and sugar. Reduce heat to medium and stir until dough is smooth, glossy and comes away from side of pan. Remove from heat. Stir 2 minutes to cool slightly. Add eggs 1 at a time. Beat after each addition until well blended. Beat in vanilla.

Drop by teaspoonfuls, a few at a time, into hot CRISCO® Shortening. Fry several minutes or until deep golden brown. Turn as needed for even browning. Remove with slotted metal spoon. Drain on paper towels. Roll in confectioners' sugar. Serve warm. *Makes 2½ dozen*

Beignets, made famous by the New Orleans French Market, are light fluffy fritter-like puffs—deep-fried until golden brown and served hot with a generous dusting of snowy confectioners' sugar.

Bourbon Street Beignet Puffs

Dinner Rolls

1¼ **cups milk**
½ **cup shortening**
3¾ **to 4¼ cups all-purpose flour, divided**
¼ **cup sugar**
2 **packages active dry yeast**
1 **teaspoon salt**
2 **eggs**

1. Combine milk and shortening in small saucepan. Heat over low heat until temperature reaches 120° to 130°F. (Shortening does not need to melt completely.) Combine 1½ cups flour, sugar, yeast and salt in large bowl. Gradually beat milk mixture into flour mixture with electric mixer at low speed. Beat in eggs and 1 cup flour. Increase speed to medium; beat 2 minutes. Stir in enough additional flour, about 1¼ cups, with wooden spoon to make soft dough.

2. Turn out dough onto lightly floured surface. Knead about 10 minutes adding enough remaining flour to make a smooth and elastic dough. Shape dough into ball; place in large, lightly greased bowl. Turn dough over so top is greased. Cover with towel; let rise in warm place 1 hour or until doubled in bulk.

3. Punch down dough. Knead on lightly floured surface 1 minute. Cover with towel; let rest 10 minutes. Grease two 8-inch square baking pans. Cut dough into halves. Cut one half into 12 pieces, keeping remaining half covered with towel. Shape pieces into balls; place in rows in 1 prepared pan. Repeat with remaining dough. Cover pans with towels; let rise in warm place 30 minutes or until doubled in bulk.

4. Preheat oven to 375°F. Bake 15 to 20 minutes or until golden brown. Remove immediately from pans. Cool on wire racks. Serve warm.

Makes 24 rolls

Dinner Rolls

Boys like this

Apple Fritters

CRISCO® Oil* for deep frying
1 egg, lightly beaten
½ cup milk
1 medium apple, peeled, cored and chopped to make 1 cup
1 tablespoon CRISCO® Oil
1 cup all-purpose flour
1 tablespoon granulated sugar
1 teaspoon baking powder
1 teaspoon ground cinnamon, divided
¼ teaspoon salt
½ cup confectioners' sugar

Use your favorite Crisco Oil product.

1. Heat 2 to 3 inches oil to 365°F in deep fryer or deep saucepan.

2. Combine egg and milk in large bowl. Stir in apple and 1 tablespoon oil.

3. Combine flour, granulated sugar, baking powder, ¼ teaspoon cinnamon and salt. Add to egg mixture. Stir until just mixed.

4. Drop by tablespoonfuls, a few at a time, into oil. Fry about 4 minutes or until golden brown. Turn as needed for even browning. Remove with slotted spoon. Drain on paper towels.

5. Combine confectioners' sugar and remaining ¾ teaspoon cinnamon in resealable bag. Gently shake fritters in mixture. Serve warm.

Makes 6 to 8 servings

PREP TIME: 15 minutes
TOTAL TIME: 25 minutes

Buttermilk Pancakes

2 cups all-purpose flour
1 tablespoon sugar
1½ teaspoons baking powder
½ teaspoon baking soda
½ teaspoon salt
1½ cups buttermilk
1 egg, beaten
¼ cup vegetable oil

1. Sift flour, sugar, baking powder, baking soda and salt into large bowl.

2. Combine buttermilk, egg and oil in medium bowl. Add liquid ingredients to dry ingredients; stir just until moistened.

3. Preheat griddle or large skillet over medium heat; grease lightly. Pour about ½ cup batter onto hot griddle for each pancake. Cook until tops of pancakes are bubbly and appear dry; turn and cook about 2 minutes or until golden. ***Makes about 12 (5-inch) pancakes***

SILVER DOLLAR PANCAKES: Use 1 tablespoon batter for each pancake. Cook as directed above.

TIP: If you don't have buttermilk on hand, use this easy substitution. Place 1 tablespoon vinegar in a measuring cup. Add milk to measure 1½ cups. Stir well; let stand 5 minutes.

Sweet Potato Biscuits

2½ cups all-purpose flour
¼ cup packed brown sugar
1 tablespoon baking powder
¾ teaspoon salt
¾ teaspoon ground cinnamon
¼ teaspoon ground ginger
¼ teaspoon ground allspice
½ cup shortening
½ cup chopped pecans
¾ cup mashed canned sweet potatoes
½ cup milk

1. Preheat oven to 450°F.

2. Combine flour, sugar, baking powder, salt, cinnamon, ginger and allspice in medium bowl. Cut in shortening with pastry blender or 2 knives until mixture resembles coarse crumbs. Stir in pecans.

3. Combine sweet potatoes and milk in separate medium bowl; mix with wire whisk until smooth.

4. Make well in center of flour mixture. Add sweet potato mixture; stir until mixture forms soft dough that clings together and forms a ball.

5. Turn out dough onto well-floured surface. Knead dough gently 10 to 12 times. Roll or pat dough to ½-inch thickness. Cut out dough with floured 2½-inch biscuit cutter.

6. Place biscuits 2 inches apart on ungreased large baking sheet. Bake 12 to 14 minutes or until tops and bottoms are golden brown. Serve warm.

Makes about 12 biscuits

Sweet Potato Biscuits

Bayou Yam Muffins

1 cup flour
1 cup yellow cornmeal
¼ cup sugar
1 tablespoon baking powder
1¼ teaspoons ground cinnamon
½ teaspoon salt
2 eggs
1 cup mashed yams or sweet potatoes
½ cup very strong cold coffee
¼ cup butter or margarine, melted
½ teaspoon TABASCO® brand Pepper Sauce

Preheat oven to 425°F. Grease 12 (3×1½-inch) muffin cups. Combine flour, cornmeal, sugar, baking powder, cinnamon and salt in large bowl. Beat eggs in medium bowl; stir in yams, coffee, butter and TABASCO® Sauce. Make a well in center of dry ingredients; add yam mixture and stir just to combine. Spoon batter into prepared muffin cups. Bake 20 to 25 minutes or until cake tester inserted in center of muffin comes out clean. Cool 5 minutes on wire rack. Remove from pans. Serve warm or at room temperature.

Makes 12 muffins

MICROWAVE DIRECTIONS: Prepare muffin batter as directed above. Spoon approximately ⅓ cup batter into each of 6 paper baking cup-lined 6-ounce custard cups or microwave-safe muffin pan cups. Cook uncovered on High (100% power) 4 to 5½ minutes or until cake tester inserted in center of muffin comes out clean; turn and rearrange cups or turn muffin pan ½ turn once during cooking. Remove muffins with small spatula. Cool 5 minutes on wire rack. Remove from pans. Repeat procedure with remaining batter. Serve warm or at room temperature.

Buttermilk Corn Bread

2 tablespoons butter
1½ cups cornmeal
½ cup all-purpose flour
1 tablespoon sugar
2 teaspoons baking powder
½ teaspoon salt
1½ cups buttermilk
½ teaspoon baking soda
2 eggs
¼ cup (½ stick) butter, melted
¼ cup chopped jalapeño peppers,* or to taste
1 tablespoon chopped pimiento

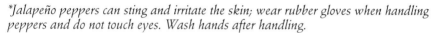

Jalapeño peppers can sting and irritate the skin; wear rubber gloves when handling peppers and do not touch eyes. Wash hands after handling.

1. Preheat oven to 425°F. Place 2 tablespoons butter in 9×2-inch deep dish pie pan or quiche pan. Place baking dish in preheated oven just before baking corn bread; heat to melt butter and coat pan.

2. Sift cornmeal, flour, sugar, baking powder and salt into large bowl; set aside. Combine buttermilk and baking soda in medium bowl. Add eggs; beat lightly with a fork. Stir in ¼ cup melted butter.

3. Add buttermilk mixture, peppers and pimiento to cornmeal mixture. Mix until just blended; do not overmix. Pour into heated baking dish. Bake 15 to 20 minutes until bread is just set. Cut into wedges.　　***Makes 8 servings***

NOTE: Corn bread should always be served hot. Do not prepare it until you are just about ready to serve dinner.

Southern Spoon Bread

4 eggs, separated
3 cups milk
1 cup yellow cornmeal
3 tablespoons butter
1 teaspoon salt
¼ teaspoon black pepper *or* **⅛ teaspoon ground red pepper**
1 teaspoon baking powder
1 tablespoon grated Parmesan cheese (optional)

1. Preheat oven to 375°F. Spray 2-quart round casserole with nonstick cooking spray; set aside. Beat egg yolks in small bowl; set aside.

2. Heat milk almost to a boil in medium saucepan over medium heat. Gradually beat in cornmeal using wire whisk. Cook 2 minutes, stirring constantly. Whisk in butter, salt and pepper. Beat about ¼ cup cornmeal mixture into egg yolks. Beat egg yolk mixture into remaining cornmeal mixture; set aside.

3. Beat egg whites in large bowl with electric mixer at high speed until stiff peaks form. Stir baking powder into cornmeal mixture. Stir about ¼ cup egg whites into cornmeal mixture. Gradually fold in remaining egg whites. Pour into prepared casserole; sprinkle with cheese, if desired.

4. Bake 30 to 35 minutes or until golden brown and toothpick inserted into center comes out clean. Serve immediately. ***Makes 6 servings***

Southern Spoon Bread

Southern Hush Puppies

CRISCO® Oil,* for frying
¾ cup yellow cornmeal
⅓ cup unsifted all-purpose flour
1½ teaspoons baking powder
½ teaspoon salt
½ cup buttermilk
1 egg
¼ cup finely chopped onion

*Use your favorite Crisco Oil product.

1. Heat 2 to 3 inches of oil in deep-fryer or large saucepan over high heat to 375°F.

2. Mix cornmeal, flour, baking powder and salt in medium mixing bowl. Add remaining ingredients; mix well.

3. Drop batter by tablespoonfuls into hot oil. Fry a few hush puppies at a time, 3 to 4 minutes, or until golden brown. Remove with slotted spoon.

4. Drain on paper towels. Repeat with remaining batter. Serve immediately or keep warm in 175°F oven.   ***Makes about 1 dozen hush puppies***

Praline French Toast

FRENCH TOAST

 1 cup EGG BEATERS®
 ⅓ cup skim milk
 1 teaspoon ground cinnamon
 1 teaspoon vanilla extract
 2 tablespoons FLEISHMANN'S® Original Margarine, divided
10 slices white bread, divided

PRALINE SAUCE

 ½ cup pecan pieces
 2 tablespoons FLEISHMANN'S® Original Margarine
 ½ cup firmly packed light brown sugar
 ½ cup maple-flavored syrup
 ⅓ cup seedless raisins

TO PREPARE FRENCH TOAST

In shallow bowl, combine Egg Beaters®, milk, cinnamon and vanilla. In large nonstick griddle or skillet, over medium heat, melt 1 tablespoon margarine. Dip half the bread slices in egg mixture to coat; transfer to griddle. Cook 2 minutes on each side or until golden. Dip remaining bread slices in egg mixture to coat. Cook using remaining margarine as needed. Keep warm.

TO PREPARE PRALINE SAUCE

In 2-quart saucepan, over medium-low heat, sauté pecans in margarine until golden. Stir in brown sugar, syrup and raisins; heat until sugar dissolves, about 5 minutes. Serve warm over French toast. ***Makes 10 servings***

Bacon and Maple Grits Puff

8 slices bacon
2 cups milk
1¼ cups water
1 cup quick-cooking grits
½ teaspoon salt
½ cup pure maple syrup
4 eggs
Fresh chives (optional)

1. Preheat oven to 350°F. Grease 1½-quart round casserole or soufflé dish; set aside.

2. Cook bacon in large skillet over medium-high heat about 7 minutes or until crisp. Remove bacon to paper towel; set aside. Reserve 2 tablespoons bacon drippings.

3. Combine milk, water, grits and salt in medium saucepan. Bring to a boil over medium heat, stirring frequently. Simmer 2 to 3 minutes or until mixture thickens, stirring constantly. Remove from heat; stir in syrup and reserved 2 tablespoons bacon drippings.

4. Crumble bacon; reserve ¼ cup for garnish. Stir remaining crumbled bacon into grits mixture.

5. Beat eggs in medium bowl. Gradually stir small amount of grits mixture into eggs. Stir egg mixture into remaining grits mixture. Pour into prepared casserole.

6. Bake 1 hour and 20 minutes or until knife inserted in center comes out clean. Top with reserved ¼ cup bacon. Garnish with fresh chives, if desired. Serve immediately. ***Makes 6 to 8 servings***

NOTE: Puff will fall slightly after removing from oven.

Bacon and Maple Grits Puff

KETTLE OF

Soups & Stews

Chicken and Sweet Potato Ragoût

2 tablespoons vegetable oil, divided
1 (3-pound) chicken, cut into 8 pieces
1 large onion, chopped
1 (14½-ounce) can chicken broth
3 small sweet potatoes, peeled and cut into ¼-inch slices
2 cups shredded green cabbage
1 tablespoon TABASCO® brand Pepper Sauce
1 teaspoon salt
¼ cup water
1 tablespoon flour
¼ cup peanut butter

Heat 1 tablespoon oil in 12-inch skillet over medium heat. Add chicken; cook until well browned. Remove to plate. Add remaining 1 tablespoon oil and onion to skillet; cook 5 minutes. Return chicken to skillet; add broth, potatoes, cabbage, TABASCO® Sauce and salt. Heat to boiling over high heat. Reduce heat to low; cover and simmer 30 minutes or until tender, stirring occasionally.

Combine water and flour in small cup. Gradually stir into skillet with peanut butter. Cook over high heat until mixture thickens. *Makes 4 servings*

Chicken and Sweet Potato Ragoût

Shrimp Jambalaya

3 tablespoons CRISCO® Stick or 3 tablespoons CRISCO®
   all-vegetable Shortening
¾ cup chopped green bell pepper, divided
½ cup chopped onion
½ cup chopped celery
⅓ cup chopped green onions
¼ pound diced cooked ham
1 clove garlic, minced
2 cups chicken broth
1 can (14½ ounces) diced tomatoes
¼ cup minced parsley
½ teaspoon salt
¼ teaspoon dried thyme leaves
⅛ teaspoon chili powder or ground red pepper
⅛ teaspoon black pepper
1 bay leaf
1 cup uncooked rice
¾ pound medium cooked shrimp, peeled and deveined

Melt CRISCO® Shortening in a large heavy skillet over medium heat. Stir in
½ cup bell pepper, onion, celery, green onions, ham and garlic. Cook for
5 minutes or until onion is tender, stirring occasionally.

Stir in chicken broth, tomatoes, parsley, salt, thyme, chili powder, pepper and
bay leaf; cover and bring to a boil. Add rice gradually stirring with a fork.

Cover and simmer for 20 minutes or until rice is tender. Mix in shrimp and
remaining ¼ cup green pepper. Simmer uncovered for 5 minutes longer.
Remove bay leaf before serving.   *Makes 6 to 8 servings*

Shrimp Jambalaya

Brunswick Stew

2 pounds chicken pieces, rinsed
2⅓ cups cold water, divided
1 can (14½ ounces) tomatoes, cut-up and undrained
2 large ribs celery, sliced
1 medium onion, chopped
2 cloves garlic, minced
1 bay leaf
½ teaspoon salt
⅛ teaspoon ground red pepper
6 small unpeeled new potatoes (about ¾ pound), cut in half
1 cup frozen succotash (about ½ of 10-ounce package)
1 cup cubed ham
1 tablespoon all-purpose flour

1. Combine chicken, 2 cups cold water, tomatoes with juice, celery, onion, garlic, bay leaf, salt and red pepper in 5-quart Dutch oven. Bring to a boil over high heat. Reduce heat to medium-low; simmer, uncovered, 45 minutes or until chicken is tender, skimming foam that rises to top.

2. Remove chicken from broth; let cool slightly. Discard bay leaf. Skim fat from soup.

3. Remove chicken meat from bones; discard skin and bones. Cut chicken into bite-size pieces.

4. Add potatoes, succotash and ham to Dutch oven. Bring to a boil. Reduce heat; simmer, uncovered, 20 minutes or until potatoes are tender. Stir in chicken.

5. Stir flour into remaining ⅓ cup cold water until smooth. Stir into stew. Cook and gently stir over medium heat until bubbly.   *Makes 6 servings*

Brunswick Stew

Dixieland Turkey Ham Creole

1 cup chopped onion
1 medium green pepper, chopped
1 (16-ounce) can stewed tomatoes, undrained
1 (8-ounce) can tomato sauce
1 teaspoon garlic salt
1 teaspoon dried thyme, crushed
   Hot pepper sauce to taste
2 cups JENNIE-O TURKEY STORE® Turkey Ham, cubed
1 (10-ounce) package frozen okra
   Hot cooked rice (optional)

In Dutch oven over medium-low heat, combine onion, green pepper, stewed tomatoes, tomato sauce, garlic salt, thyme and hot pepper sauce. Cover and simmer 20 minutes, stirring occasionally. Stir in turkey ham and okra; cover and cook 10 minutes longer or until okra is tender, stirring occasionally. Serve over hot cooked rice, if desired.   *Makes 6 servings*

PREP TIME: 15 minutes
COOK TIME: 30 minutes

Red Bean Soup with Andouille Sausage

2 tablespoons butter
1 large sweet onion, diced
3 stalks celery, diced
2 large cloves garlic, chopped
1 ham hock
8 cups chicken broth
1½ cups dried red kidney beans, soaked in cold water 1 hour,
   rinsed and drained
1 bay leaf
2 parsnips, diced
1 sweet potato, diced
1 pound andouille smoked sausage or other pork sausage,
   cut into ½-inch pieces
Salt and black pepper

SLOW COOKER DIRECTIONS

1. Melt butter in large saucepan over medium heat. Add onion, celery and garlic. Cook and stir 5 minutes. Place in slow cooker. Add ham hock, broth, kidney beans and bay leaf. Cover; cook on HIGH 2 hours.

2. Remove ham hock; discard. Add parsnips and sweet potato. Cover; cook an additional 2 hours.

3. Add sausage. Cover; cook 30 minutes or until heated through. Remove and discard bay leaf. Season with salt and pepper.   *Makes 6 to 8 servings*

NOTE: Use a 6-quart slow cooker for this recipe. If using a smaller slow cooker, cut the recipe ingredients in half.

Hoppin' John Soup

4 strips uncooked bacon, chopped
1 large onion, chopped
2 cloves garlic, minced
2 cans (15 ounces each) black-eyed peas, undrained
1 can (14½ ounces) reduced-sodium chicken broth
3 to 4 tablespoons *Frank's® RedHot® Original Cayenne Pepper Sauce*
1 teaspoon dried thyme leaves
1 bay leaf
2 cups cooked long-grain rice (¾ cup uncooked rice)
2 tablespoons minced fresh parsley

1. Cook bacon, onion and garlic in large saucepan over medium-high heat 5 minutes or until vegetables are tender.

2. Add peas with liquid, broth, *½ cup water,* **Frank's RedHot** Sauce, thyme and bay leaf. Bring to a boil. Reduce heat to low; cook, covered, 15 minutes, stirring occasionally. Remove and discard bay leaf.

3. Combine rice and parsley in medium bowl. Spoon rice evenly into 6 serving bowls. Ladle soup over rice. *Makes 6 servings*

NOTE: For an attractive presentation, pack rice mixture into small ramekin dishes. Unmold into soup bowls. Ladle soup around rice.

PREP TIME: 15 minutes
COOK TIME: 20 minutes

Hoppin' John Soup

Spicy Shrimp Gumbo

½ cup vegetable oil
½ cup all-purpose flour
 1 large onion, chopped
½ cup chopped fresh parsley
½ cup chopped celery
½ cup sliced green onions
 6 cloves garlic, minced
 4 cups chicken broth or water*
 1 package (10 ounces) frozen sliced okra, thawed
 1 teaspoon salt
½ teaspoon ground red pepper
 2 pounds raw medium shrimp, peeled and deveined
 3 cups hot cooked rice
   Fresh parsley sprigs for garnish

Traditional gumbo is thick like stew. For thinner gumbo, add 1 to 2 cups additional broth.

1. For roux, blend oil and flour in large heavy stockpot. Cook over medium heat 10 to 15 minutes or until roux is dark brown but not burned, stirring often.

2. Add chopped onion, chopped parsley, celery, green onions and garlic to roux. Cook over medium heat 5 to 10 minutes or until vegetables are tender. Add broth, okra, salt and red pepper. Cover; simmer 15 minutes.

3. Add shrimp; simmer 3 to 5 minutes or until shrimp turn pink and opaque.

4. Place about ⅓ cup rice into 8 wide-rimmed soup bowls; top with gumbo. Garnish, if desired.   *Makes 8 servings*

Spicy Shrimp Gumbo

Corn and Tomato Chowder

1½ cups peeled and diced plum tomatoes
¾ teaspoon salt, divided
2 ears corn, husks removed
1 tablespoon butter
½ cup finely chopped shallots
1 clove garlic, minced
1 can (12 ounces) evaporated skimmed milk
1 cup chicken broth
1 tablespoon finely chopped fresh sage *or* 1 teaspoon rubbed sage
¼ teaspoon black pepper
1 tablespoon cornstarch
2 tablespoons cold water

1. Place tomatoes in nonmetal colander over bowl. Sprinkle with ½ teaspoon salt; toss to mix well. Allow tomatoes to drain at least 1 hour.

2. Meanwhile, cut corn kernels off cobs into small bowl. Scrape cobs with dull side of knife to extract liquid from cobs into same bowl; set aside. Discard 1 cob; break remaining cob in half.

3. Heat butter in heavy medium saucepan over medium-high heat until melted and bubbly. Add shallots and garlic; reduce heat to low. Cover and cook about 5 minutes or until shallots are soft and translucent. Add milk, broth, sage, pepper and reserved corn cob halves. Bring to a boil over high heat. Reduce heat to low; simmer, uncovered, 10 minutes. Remove and discard cob halves.

4. Add corn with liquid; return to a boil over medium-high heat. Reduce heat to low; simmer, uncovered, 15 minutes more. Dissolve cornstarch in water; add to chowder. Stir until thickened. Remove from heat; stir in drained tomatoes and remaining ¼ teaspoon salt. Spoon into bowls. Garnish with additional fresh sage, if desired. *Makes 4 servings*

Corn and Tomato Chowder

Sausage and Chicken Gumbo

1 tablespoon oil
1 red bell pepper, chopped
1 pound boneless skinless chicken thigh meat, trimmed
    of excess fat and cut into 1-inch pieces
1 package (12 ounces) Cajun andouille flavor chicken sausage,
    sliced ½ inch thick
½ cup chicken broth
1 can (28 ounces) crushed tomatoes with roasted garlic
¼ cup finely chopped green onions
1 bay leaf
½ teaspoon dried basil leaves
½ teaspoon black pepper
¼ to ½ teaspoon red pepper flakes
6 lemon wedges

1. Heat oil in large saucepan. Add bell pepper; cook and stir over high heat 2 to 3 minutes. Add chicken; cook and stir about 2 minutes or until browned. Add sausage; cook and stir 2 minutes or until browned. Add broth; scrape up any browned bits from bottom of saucepan.

2. Add tomatoes, green onions, bay leaf, basil, black pepper and red pepper flakes. Simmer 15 minutes. Remove and discard bay leaf. Garnish each serving with lemon wedge.   *Makes 6 servings*

Oyster Stew

1 quart shucked oysters, with their liquor
8 cups milk
8 tablespoons margarine, cut into pieces
1 teaspoon freshly ground white pepper
½ teaspoon salt
   Paprika
2 tablespoons finely chopped fresh parsley

Heat oysters in their liquor in medium saucepan over high heat until oyster edges begin to curl, about 2 to 3 minutes. Heat milk and margarine together in large saucepan over medium-high heat just to boiling. Add pepper and salt.

Stir in oysters and their liquor. Do not boil or overcook stew or oysters may get tough. Pour stew into tureen. Dust with paprika; sprinkle with parsley.

Makes 8 servings

Favorite recipe from **National Fisheries Institute**

When purchasing shucked oysters, look for ones that are plump, uniform in size and have good color. The liquor (liquid) should be clear and they should smell like the sea. Shucked oysters can be stored, covered by their liquor, for up to 2 days in the refrigerator or up to 3 months in the freezer.

Greens, White Bean and Barley Soup

½ pound carrots, peeled
2 tablespoons olive oil
1½ cups chopped onions
2 cloves garlic, minced
1½ cups sliced button mushrooms
6 cups vegetable broth
2 cups cooked barley
1 can (15 ounces) Great Northern beans, rinsed and drained
2 bay leaves
1 teaspoon sugar
1 teaspoon dried thyme leaves
1½ pounds collard greens, washed, stemmed and chopped
  (about 7 cups)
1 tablespoon white wine vinegar
Hot pepper sauce
Red bell pepper strips for garnish

1. Cut carrots lengthwise into quarters; cut crosswise into ¼-inch pieces. Heat oil in Dutch oven over medium heat until hot. Add carrots, onions and garlic; cook and stir 3 minutes. Add mushrooms; cook and stir 5 minutes or until tender.

2. Add broth, barley, beans, bay leaves, sugar and thyme. Bring to a boil over high heat. Reduce heat to low. Cover and simmer 5 minutes. Add greens; simmer 10 minutes. Remove bay leaves; discard. Stir in vinegar. Season to taste with pepper sauce. Garnish, if desired.

Makes 8 (1¼-cup) servings

Greens, White Bean and Barley Soup

New Orleans Pork Gumbo

1 pound pork tenderloin
  Nonstick cooking spray
1 tablespoon butter
2 tablespoons all-purpose flour
1 cup water
1 can (16 ounces) stewed tomatoes, undrained
1 package (10 ounces) frozen cut okra
1 package (10 ounces) frozen succotash
1 beef bouillon cube
1 teaspoon black pepper
1 teaspoon hot pepper sauce
1 bay leaf

1. Cut pork into ½-inch cubes. Spray large Dutch oven with cooking spray. Heat over medium heat until hot. Add pork; cook and stir 4 minutes or until pork is browned. Remove pork from Dutch oven.

2. Melt butter in same Dutch oven. Stir in flour. Cook and stir until mixture is browned. Gradually whisk in water until smooth. Add pork and remaining ingredients. Bring to a boil. Reduce heat to low; simmer 15 minutes. Remove bay leaf before serving. ***Makes 4 servings***

PREP AND COOK TIME: 30 minutes

Charleston Crab Soup

2 tablespoons butter
½ cup finely chopped onion
1 tablespoon plus 1½ teaspoons all-purpose flour
1 cup bottled clam juice or chicken broth
2½ cups half-and-half
8 ounces lump crabmeat
1½ teaspoons Worcestershire sauce
½ teaspoon salt
Dash ground white pepper
1 to 2 tablespoons dry sherry

1. Melt butter in medium saucepan over medium-low heat. Add onion; cook and stir 4 minutes or until tender. Stir in flour; cook and stir 1 minute.

2. Add clam juice; cook and stir over medium heat until mixture comes to a simmer. Add half-and-half, crab, Worcestershire sauce, salt and pepper. Cook and stir over low heat 3 to 4 minutes just until mixture begins to simmer, stirring occasionally. Remove from heat; stir in sherry.

Makes 4 to 5 servings

Southern Secret

To make authentic she-crab soup, add crab roe (eggs) to the soup. If these are not available, substitute crumbled hard-boiled egg yolks. To serve, place a small amount of roe or crumbled egg yolks on the bottom of each bowl. Ladle soup over the roe or egg yolks.

Smoked Sausage Gumbo

1 can (14½ ounces) diced tomatoes, undrained
1 cup chicken broth
¼ cup all-purpose flour
2 tablespoons olive oil
¾ pound Polish sausage, cut into ½-inch pieces
1 medium onion, diced
1 green bell pepper, diced
2 ribs celery, chopped
1 carrot, peeled and chopped
2 teaspoons dried oregano leaves
2 teaspoons dried thyme leaves
⅛ teaspoon ground red pepper
   Hot cooked rice
   Chopped parsley (optional)

SLOW COOKER DIRECTIONS

1. Combine tomatoes with juice and broth in slow cooker. Sprinkle flour evenly over bottom of small skillet. Cook over high heat without stirring 3 to 4 minutes or until flour begins to brown. Reduce heat to medium; stir flour about 4 minutes. Stir in oil until smooth. Carefully whisk flour mixture into slow cooker.

2. Add sausage, onion, bell pepper, celery, carrot, oregano, thyme and red pepper to slow cooker. Stir well. Cover; cook on LOW 4½ to 5 hours or until thickened.

3. Serve gumbo over rice. Sprinkle with parsley, if desired.

Makes 4 servings

TIP: If gumbo thickens too much upon standing, stir in additional broth.

Smoked Sausage Gumbo

Shrimp Étouffée

   3 tablespoons oil
¼ cup all-purpose flour
   1 cup chopped onion
   1 cup chopped green bell pepper
½ cup chopped carrot
½ cup chopped celery
   4 cloves garlic, minced
   1 can (14½ ounces) clear vegetable broth
   1 bottle (8 ounces) clam juice
½ teaspoon salt
2½ pounds uncooked large shrimp, peeled and deveined
   1 teaspoon red pepper flakes
   1 teaspoon hot pepper sauce
   4 cups hot cooked white or basmati rice
½ cup chopped flat leaf parsley
     Additional hot pepper sauce (optional)

1. Heat oil in Dutch oven over medium heat. Add flour; cook and stir 10 to 15 minutes or until flour mixture is deep golden brown. Add onion, bell pepper, carrot, celery and garlic; cook and stir 5 minutes.

2. Stir in broth, clam juice and salt; bring to a boil. Simmer, uncovered, 10 minutes or until vegetables are tender. Stir in shrimp, red pepper flakes and hot pepper sauce; simmer 6 to 8 minutes or until shrimp are opaque.

3. Ladle into 8 shallow bowls; top each with ½ cup rice. Sprinkle with parsley. Serve with additional pepper sauce, if desired.   *Makes 8 servings*

Shrimp Étouffée

Chicken Gumbo

2 tablespoons all-purpose flour
2 teaspoons blackened seasoning mix or Creole seasoning mix
¾ pound boneless skinless chicken thighs, cut into ¾-inch pieces
2 teaspoons olive oil
1 large onion, coarsely chopped
½ cup sliced celery
2 teaspoons minced garlic
1 can (14½ ounces) chicken broth
1 can (14½ ounces) stewed tomatoes, undrained
1 large green bell pepper, cut into chunks
1 teaspoon filé powder (optional)
2 cups hot cooked rice
2 tablespoons chopped fresh parsley

1. Combine flour and blackened seasoning mix in large resealable plastic food storage bag. Add chicken; toss to coat. Heat oil in large deep nonstick skillet or saucepan over medium heat. Add chicken to skillet; sprinkle with any remaining flour mixture. Cook and stir 3 minutes. Add onion, celery and garlic; cook and stir 3 minutes.

2. Add broth, tomatoes with juice and bell pepper; bring to a boil. Reduce heat; cover and simmer 20 minutes or until vegetables are tender. Uncover; simmer 5 to 10 minutes or until sauce is slightly reduced. Remove from heat; stir in filé powder, if desired. Ladle into shallow bowls; top with rice and parsley.

Makes 4 servings

NOTE: Filé powder, made from dried sassafras leaves, thickens and adds flavor to gumbos. Look for it in the herb and spice section of your supermarket.

PREP TIME: 15 minutes
COOK TIME: 40 minutes

Chicken Gumbo

Double Corn Chowder with Sausage

1 package JENNIE-O TURKEY STORE® Lean Turkey Bratwurst
1 cup chopped onion
1 can (15 ounces) cream-style corn
2 cups half-and-half or whole milk
1 cup fresh or frozen corn kernels
½ cup finely diced red or green bell pepper
¼ teaspoon freshly ground black pepper
¼ teaspoon hot pepper sauce
½ cup seasoned croutons
   Chopped chives or green onion tops (optional)

Crumble bratwurst into large saucepan; discard casings. Add onion; cook over medium heat 8 minutes, breaking up bratwurst into chunks. Add creamed corn, half-and-half, corn kernels, bell pepper, black pepper and hot pepper sauce. Simmer uncovered 15 minutes, stirring occasionally. Ladle into soup bowls; top with croutons and chives, if desired.   *Makes 6 servings*

*Chowder is a thick chunky soup usually made
with cream or milk. Be sure to simmer, not boil, the
soup to prevent the cream from curdling.*

Peanut Soup

2 tablespoons butter
2 tablespoons grated onion
1 stalk celery, thinly sliced
2 tablespoons flour
3 cups chicken broth
½ cup creamy peanut butter
2 tablespoons dry sherry
2 teaspoons lemon juice
¼ teaspoon salt
2 tablespoons chopped dry roasted peanuts

In medium sauce pan, melt butter over medium heat. Add onion and celery and sauté 5 minutes. Stir in flour and mix until well blended. Gradually stir in chicken broth. Stirring to keep mixture smooth, simmer 30 minutes. Remove from heat and strain. Return liquid to heat and stir in peanut butter, sherry, lemon juice and salt. Heat through and serve garnished with chopped peanuts. *Makes 4 to 6 servings*

Favorite recipe from **Peanut Advisory Board**

Shrimp and Fish Gumbo

8 ounces fresh or frozen orange roughy or other fish fillets

3¾ cups water, divided

6 ounces deveined shelled raw shrimp

1 cup chopped onion

½ cup chopped green bell pepper

2 cloves garlic, minced

½ teaspoon chicken or fish bouillon granules

2 cans (14½ ounces each) stewed tomatoes, undrained

1½ cups frozen okra, thawed

1 teaspoon dried thyme leaves

1 teaspoon dried savory leaves

¼ teaspoon ground red pepper

⅛ teaspoon black pepper

2 tablespoons cornstarch

2 tablespoons finely chopped ham

2 cups hot cooked brown rice

1. Remove and discard skin from fish; cut fish into 1-inch pieces. Bring 3 cups water to a boil in medium saucepan over high heat. Add fish and shrimp; cook 3 to 4 minutes or until fish flakes easily when tested with fork and shrimp are opaque. Drain; set aside. Combine onion, bell pepper, additional ½ cup water, garlic and bouillon granules in large saucepan. Bring to a boil over medium-high heat; reduce to medium-low. Cover; simmer 2 to 3 minutes or until vegetables are crisp-tender.

2. Stir in tomatoes with juice, okra, thyme, savory, red pepper and black pepper. Return to a boil; reduce heat. Simmer, uncovered, 3 to 5 minutes or until okra is tender. Combine remaining ¼ cup water and cornstarch in small bowl. Stir into gumbo. Cook and stir over medium heat until mixture boils and thickens. Cook and stir 2 minutes more. Add fish, shrimp and ham; heat through. Serve over rice. *Makes 4 servings*

Shrimp and Fish Gumbo

HERITAGE
Meats & Poultry

Southern Buttermilk Fried Chicken

        3 pounds chicken pieces
        2 cups all-purpose flour
    1½ teaspoons celery salt
        1 teaspoon dried thyme leaves
        ¾ teaspoon black pepper
        ½ teaspoon dried marjoram leaves
    1¾ cups buttermilk

1. Rinse chicken; pat dry with paper towels. Combine flour, celery salt, thyme, pepper and marjoram in shallow bowl. Pour buttermilk into medium bowl.

2. Heat 2 cups vegetable oil in large cast iron or heavy deep skillet over medium heat until oil reaches 340°F on deep fat thermometer.

3. Dip half the chicken in buttermilk, one piece at a time; shake off excess buttermilk. Coat with flour mixture; shake off excess. Dip again in buttermilk, then coat with flour mixture. Fry chicken, skin side down, 10 to 12 minutes or until brown. Turn and fry 12 to 14 minutes or until brown and juices run clear. Drain on paper towels. Repeat with remaining chicken, buttermilk and flour mixture. *Makes 4 servings*

Southern Buttermilk Fried Chicken

Memphis Pork Ribs

1 tablespoon chili powder
1 tablespoon dried parsley
2 teaspoons onion powder
2 teaspoons garlic powder
2 teaspoons dried oregano leaves
2 teaspoons paprika
2 teaspoons black pepper
1½ teaspoons salt
4 pounds pork spareribs, cut into 4 racks
Tennessee BBQ Sauce (page 86)

1. Combine chili powder, parsley, onion powder, garlic powder, oregano, paprika, pepper and salt in small bowl; mix well.

2. Rub spice mixture onto ribs. Cover; marinate in refrigerator 2 hours or overnight.

3. Preheat oven to 350°F. Place ribs in foil-lined shallow roasting pan. Bake 45 minutes.

4. Meanwhile, prepare grill for direct cooking. Prepare Tennessee BBQ sauce. Reserve 1 cup sauce for dipping.

5. Place ribs on grid. Grill, covered, over medium heat 10 minutes. Brush with sauce. Continue grilling 10 minutes or until ribs are tender, brushing with sauce occasionally. Serve reserved sauce for dipping.

Makes 4 servings

Memphis Pork Ribs

Tennessee BBQ Sauce

3 cups prepared barbecue sauce
¼ cup cider vinegar
¼ cup honey
2 teaspoons onion powder
2 teaspoons garlic powder
   Dash hot pepper sauce

Combine all ingredients in medium bowl; mix well.

Makes about 3½ cups

Carolina Baked Beans & Pork Chops

2 cans (16 ounces each) pork and beans
½ cup chopped onion
½ cup chopped green bell pepper
¼ cup *French's® Classic Yellow®* Mustard
¼ cup packed light brown sugar
2 tablespoons *French's®* Worcestershire Sauce
1 tablespoon *Frank's® RedHot®* Original Cayenne Pepper Sauce
6 boneless pork chops (1 inch thick)

1. Preheat oven to 400°F. Combine all ingredients *except pork chops* in 3-quart shallow baking dish; mix well. Arrange chops on top, turning once to coat with sauce.

2. Bake, uncovered, 30 to 35 minutes or until pork is no longer pink in center. Stir beans around chops once during baking. Serve with green beans or mashed potatoes, if desired. *Makes 6 servings*

PREP TIME: 10 minutes
COOK TIME: 30 minutes

Carolina Baked Beans & Pork Chop

Muffuletta

1 (9¾-ounce) jar green olive salad, drained and chopped
¼ cup pitted black olives, chopped
1 large stalk celery, finely chopped
1½ teaspoons TABASCO® brand Pepper Sauce, divided
1 (8-inch) round loaf crusty French or sourdough bread
3 tablespoons olive oil
4 ounces sliced salami
4 ounces sliced baked ham
4 ounces sliced provolone cheese

Combine green olive salad, black olives, celery and 1 teaspoon TABASCO®
Sauce in medium bowl. Cut bread crosswise in half; remove some of soft
inside from each half. Combine oil and remaining ½ teaspoon TABASCO®
Sauce in small bowl. Brush mixture on inside of bread. Fill bottom with olive
mixture. Top with salami, ham and provolone slices. Top with remaining
bread half. Cut loaf into quarters.   *Makes 4 to 6 servings*

*Muffulettas are usually served cold; however,
they are also delicious hot. To heat Muffulettas, preheat
the oven to 350°F. Place the sandwiches on the oven
rack before cutting. Heat 10 minutes or until the
cheese is melted.*

Muffuletta

Kentucky Burgoo Pie

BURGOO FILLING

1½ pounds chicken, skinned
½ pound beef stew meat
½ pound pork shoulder roast
½ pound veal shoulder roast
1½ cups water
2 carrots, peeled and sliced
2 potatoes, peeled and cubed
2 tomatoes, peeled and chopped
1 rib celery, chopped
1 medium onion, chopped
1 small green bell pepper, chopped
1 cup fresh or drained canned butter beans or lima beans
1 cup fresh or frozen whole kernel corn
½ cup tomato juice
1 can (10½ ounces) tomato purée
1 tablespoon salt
1½ teaspoons hot pepper sauce
1½ teaspoons Worcestershire sauce
1 teaspoon black pepper
½ teaspoon ground red pepper

CRUST

1 (10-inch) Classic CRISCO® Double Crust (page 166)

SAUCE

⅓ cup butter or margarine
⅓ cup all-purpose flour
½ teaspoon salt
¼ teaspoon black pepper
⅔ cup milk

DECORATIONS

1 (9-inch) Classic CRISCO® Single Crust (page 155)

1. For filling, combine chicken, beef, pork, veal and water in 5-quart Dutch oven. Cover and simmer, turning meat frequently, until tender, about 1½ to 2 hours. Add additional water, if necessary. Drain, reserving liquid; cool. Debone meat; cut into ¼-inch cubes. Place meat and reserved liquid in large container. Refrigerate several hours or overnight. Skim off and discard fat from surface.

2. Place meat and liquid in Dutch oven. Add carrots, potatoes, tomatoes, celery, onion, green pepper, butter beans, corn, tomato juice, tomato purée, 1 tablespoon salt, pepper sauce, Worcestershire sauce, 1 teaspoon black pepper and red pepper to Dutch oven. Simmer, covered, 1 hour. Uncover; simmer 2 hours. Remove from heat.

3. Prepare 10-inch crust. Divide dough in half. Roll and press bottom crust into 10-inch pie plate or 1½-quart casserole. *Do not bake.* Heat oven to 425°F.

4. For sauce, melt butter in medium saucepan. Stir in flour, ½ teaspoon salt and ¼ teaspoon black pepper. Cook and stir until bubbly. Remove from heat. Stir in milk. Return to heat; cook and stir 1 minute. Remove from heat. Stir in small amount of filling. Continue adding small amounts of filling until mixture in saucepan measures about 2 cups. Return to Dutch oven. Stir to blend. Spoon 3½ cups filling into unbaked pie crust. (Refrigerate or freeze remaining thickened filling for additional pie.) Moisten pastry edge with water.

5. Roll out top crust. Lift onto filled pie. Trim ½ inch beyond edge of pie plate. Fold top edge under bottom crust. *Do not flute.*

6. For decorations, prepare 9-inch crust. Roll dough into 10×8-inch rectangle. Cut 12 (⅜-inch) strips and 4 leaf shapes from crust. Braid strips. Moisten edge of top crust with water. Place braids on edge of pie. Moisten underside of leaves. Arrange on top of crust. Cut slits or shapes into top to allow steam to escape.

7. Bake at 425°F for 30 to 35 minutes. *Do not overbake.* Serve warm. Refrigerate leftover pie.   *Makes one 10-inch pie*

Deep South Ham and Redeye Gravy

1 tablespoon butter
1 ham steak (about 1⅓ pounds)
1 cup strong coffee
¾ teaspoon sugar
¼ teaspoon hot pepper sauce

1. Heat large skillet over medium-high heat until hot. Add butter; tilt skillet to coat bottom. Add ham steak; cook 3 minutes. Turn; cook 2 minutes longer or until lightly browned. Remove ham to serving platter; set aside and keep warm.

2. Add coffee, sugar and pepper sauce to same skillet. Bring to a boil over high heat; boil 2 to 3 minutes or until liquid is reduced to ¼ cup, scraping up any brown bits. Serve gravy over ham.   *Makes 4 servings*

SERVING SUGGESTION: Serve ham steak with sautéed greens and poached eggs.

Deep South Ham and Redeye Gravy

Classic Fried Chicken

¾ **cup all-purpose flour**
1 **teaspoon salt**
¼ **teaspoon pepper**
1 **frying chicken (2½ to 3 pounds), cut up**
½ **cup CRISCO® Oil***

*Use your favorite Crisco Oil product.

1. Combine flour, salt and pepper in paper or plastic bag. Add a few pieces of chicken at a time. Shake to coat.

2. Heat oil to 365°F in electric skillet or on medium-high heat in large heavy skillet. Fry chicken 30 to 40 minutes without lowering heat until no longer pink in center. Turn once for even browning. Drain on paper towels.

Makes 4 servings

TIP: For thicker crust, increase flour to 1½ cups. Shake damp chicken in seasoned flour. Place on waxed paper. Let stand for 5 to 20 minutes before frying.

SPICY FRIED CHICKEN: Increase pepper to ½ teaspoon. Combine pepper with ½ teaspoon poultry seasoning, ½ teaspoon paprika, ½ teaspoon cayenne pepper and ¼ teaspoon dry mustard. Rub on chicken before step 1. Substitute 2¼ teaspoons garlic salt, ¼ teaspoon salt and ¼ teaspoon celery salt for 1 teaspoon salt. Combine with flour in step 1 and proceed as directed above.

BBQ Short Ribs with Cola Sauce

1 large (17×15 inches) foil bag
1 can (12 ounces) regular cola
1 can (6 ounces) tomato paste
¾ cup honey
½ cup cider vinegar
1 teaspoon salt
2 cloves garlic, minced
  Dash hot pepper sauce (optional)
4 pounds beef short ribs, cut into 2-inch lengths

1. Preheat oven to 450°F. Place foil bag in 1-inch-deep jelly-roll pan. Spray inside of bag with nonstick cooking spray. Dust with flour.

2. To prepare sauce, combine cola, tomato paste, honey, vinegar, salt, garlic and hot pepper sauce, if desired, in 2-quart saucepan. Bring to a boil over medium-high heat. Reduce heat to medium and cook, stirring occasionally, until slightly reduced, about 15 minutes.

3. Dip each short rib in sauce. Place ribs in single layer in prepared foil bag. Ladle additional 1 cup sauce into bag. Seal bag; leave headspace for heat circulation by folding open end twice.

4. Bake 1 hour 15 minutes or until ribs are cooked through. Carefully cut open bag. *Makes 4 to 6 servings*

Southern Secret

Beef short ribs can be purchased bone in or boneless. Purchase ⅓ or ½ pounds per person for bone in short ribs. For boneless short ribs purchase ¼ to ⅓ pounds per person. Short ribs are a less tender cut that need moist heat cooking. After long, slow cooking, they are juicy and delicious.

Roast Beef Po' Boy

6 tablespoons butter or margarine
6 tablespoons flour
1½ cups sliced onion (1 large)
1 small green bell pepper, sliced (1 cup)
2 cups beef broth
1 teaspoon Worcestershire sauce
1 teaspoon TABASCO® brand Pepper Sauce
½ teaspoon dried thyme leaves
4 (6-inch) French or round rolls
1 pound thinly sliced cooked beef

Melt butter in medium saucepan over medium heat; stir in flour. Cook about 4 minutes or until flour browns, stirring constantly. Add onion and green bell pepper; cook and stir about 5 minutes. Gradually stir in broth. Add Worcestershire sauce, TABASCO® Sauce and thyme; cook and stir until mixture boils and thickens.

Cut thin slice from top of each roll. Scoop out soft insides; fill with beef. Spoon gravy over beef. Replace tops on rolls. *Makes 4 sandwiches*

Newman's Own® Pecan Chicken
with Brandied Peach Salsa

⅓ **cup gingersnap crumbs (about 6 cookies)**
⅓ **cup pecans, ground**
4 **boneless skinless, chicken breast halves**
1 **tablespoon Dijon mustard**
1 **(16-ounce) jar NEWMAN'S OWN® Peach Salsa**
2 **tablespoons peach brandy**
¼ **cup toasted pecan halves for garnish***

*To toast pecan halves, place in shallow pan in oven for the last 5 minutes that the chicken is baking.

Preheat oven to 425°F. Spray rack in broiling pan with nonstick cooking spray.

Combine gingersnap crumbs and ground pecans in shallow dish. Brush chicken with mustard, then dredge with crumb-nut mixture, coating all sides. Place chicken on rack in broiling pan. Bake chicken 20 minutes.

Meanwhile, in small saucepan heat salsa and peach brandy over medium heat 5 minutes or until heated through.

To serve, place chicken on platter. Spoon hot peach salsa over and around chicken. Garnish with pecan halves. *Makes 4 servings*

Creole Red Beans and Rice

1 cup uncooked dried red kidney beans
2 green bell peppers, diced
1 can (14½ ounces) original-style stewed tomatoes, undrained
1¾ cups chicken broth
1 cup chopped onion
2 ribs celery, diced
¼ cup water
1 tablespoon Worcestershire sauce
3 cloves garlic, minced
2 bay leaves
1 teaspoon Creole seasoning
⅛ teaspoon ground cinnamon
⅛ teaspoon ground cloves
⅛ teaspoon ground red pepper
½ pound andouille sausage, sliced
1 cup uncooked white rice

1. Rinse beans thoroughly in colander under cold running water. Place in medium saucepan; cover with 4 inches water. Bring to a boil over high heat; boil 2 minutes. Remove from heat. Cover; let stand 1 hour. Drain well.

2. Preheat oven to 350°F.

3. Combine remaining ingredients except sausage and rice in Dutch oven. Bring to a boil over high heat; add sausage and beans.

4. Cover Dutch oven tightly with foil. Bake 1½ hours or until beans are tender. Remove from oven; discard bay leaves. Let stand 10 minutes before serving.

5. Meanwhile, cook rice according to package directions; keep warm.

6. To serve, divide rice evenly among 4 serving dishes; top with bean mixture. Garnish, if desired.   *Makes 4 servings*

Creole Red Beans and Rice

Southern Barbecue Sandwich

1 pound boneless beef top sirloin or flank steak*
¾ cup *French's®* Worcestershire Sauce, divided
½ cup ketchup
½ cup light molasses
¼ cup *French's®* Classic Yellow® Mustard
2 tablespoons *Frank's® RedHot®* Original Cayenne Pepper Sauce
½ teaspoon hickory salt
4 sandwich buns, split

*You can substitute 1 pound pork tenderloin for the steak. Cook pork until meat is juicy and barely pink in center or substitute leftover sliced steak for the grilled steak. Stir into sauce and heat through.

1. Place steak in large resealable plastic food storage bag. Pour ½ cup Worcestershire over steak. Seal bag and marinate meat in refrigerator 20 minutes.

2. To prepare barbecue sauce, combine ketchup, molasses, remaining ¼ cup Worcestershire, mustard, **Frank's RedHot** Sauce and hickory salt in medium saucepan. Bring to a boil over high heat. Reduce heat to low. Cook 5 minutes until slightly thickened, stirring occasionally. Set aside.

3. Place steak on grid, discarding marinade. Grill over hot coals 15 minutes, turning once. Remove steak from grid; let stand 5 minutes. Cut steak diagonally into thin slices. Stir meat into barbecue sauce. Cook until heated through, stirring often. Serve steak and sauce in sandwich buns. Garnish as desired.

Makes 4 servings

PREP TIME: 15 minutes
MARINATE TIME: 20 minutes
COOK TIME: 25 minutes

Southern Barbecue Sandwich

Biscuits 'n Gravy

BISCUITS

PAM® No-Stick Cooking Spray
2 cups self-rising flour
2 teaspoons granulated sugar
1½ teaspoons baking powder
1 cup buttermilk
¼ cup WESSON® Vegetable Oil

GRAVY

1 pound bulk pork sausage
¼ cup all-purpose flour
2 cups milk
¼ teaspoon salt
¼ teaspoon ground black pepper

BISCUITS

1. **Spray** a baking sheet with cooking spray. Combine flour, sugar and baking powder in a large bowl; blend well. Whisk together buttermilk and oil in a small bowl; add to dry ingredients and mix until dough is moist but not sticky.

2. **Knead** dough lightly 5 times on a lightly floured surface. Roll dough to a ¾-inch thickness; cut with a 4-inch biscuit cutter. Knead any scraps together and repeat cutting method. Place biscuits on baking sheet; bake in preheated 450°F oven for 10 to 15 minutes or until golden brown. Keep warm.

GRAVY

3. **Cook** and crumble sausage in a large skillet until brown. Reserve ¼ cup of drippings in skillet; drain sausage well. Set aside. Add flour to drippings in skillet; whisk until smooth. Cook over medium heat for 2 to 3 minutes or until dark brown, stirring constantly. Gradually add milk, stirring constantly until smooth and thickened. Stir in salt, pepper and sausage; heat through. Split warm biscuits in half; ladle gravy over biscuits. *Makes 8 servings*

Sausage and Cheese Grits

PAM® No-Stick Cooking Spray
1 pound mild or hot sausage, cooked, crumbled and drained
4½ cups water
¼ teaspoon salt
1½ cups grits
2½ cups shredded Cheddar cheese
3 tablespoons WESSON® Vegetable Oil
1½ cups milk
3 eggs, slightly beaten

1. **Spray** a 13×9×2-inch baking dish with cooking spray. Spread cooked sausage in dish; set aside.

2. **Bring** water and salt to a boil in a large saucepan. Stir in grits; reduce heat. Cook 5 minutes or until thickened, stirring occasionally. Add cheese and oil; stir until cheese has melted. Stir in milk and eggs; blend well. **Spoon grits over sausage.**

3. **Bake**, uncovered, in a preheated 350°F oven 1 hour or until grits have set.

Makes 10 servings

PREP TIME: 15 minutes
COOK TIME: 1 hour

Carolina-Style Barbecue Chicken

2 pounds boneless skinless chicken breast halves or thighs
¾ cup packed light brown sugar, divided
¾ cup *French's*® Classic Yellow® Mustard
½ cup cider vinegar
¼ cup *Frank's*® *RedHot*® Original Cayenne Pepper Sauce
2 tablespoons vegetable oil
2 tablespoons *French's*® Worcestershire Sauce
½ teaspoon salt
¼ teaspoon black pepper

1. Place chicken in large resealable plastic food storage bag. Combine ½ cup brown sugar, mustard, vinegar, ***Frank's RedHot*** Sauce, oil, Worcestershire, salt and pepper in 4-cup measure; mix well. Pour 1 cup mustard mixture over chicken. Seal bag; marinate in refrigerator 1 hour or overnight.

2. Pour remaining mustard mixture into small saucepan. Stir in remaining ¼ cup brown sugar. Bring to a boil. Reduce heat; simmer 5 minutes or until sugar dissolves and mixture thickens slightly, stirring often. Reserve for serving sauce.

3. Place chicken on well-oiled grid, reserving marinade. Grill over high heat 10 to 15 minutes or until chicken is no longer pink in center, turning and basting once with marinade. *Do not baste during last 5 minutes of cooking.* Discard any remaining marinade. Serve chicken with reserved sauce.

Makes 8 servings

PREP TIME: 15 minutes
MARINATE TIME: 1 hour
COOK TIME: 10 minutes

Carolina-Style Barbecue Chicken

Peach-Glazed Virginia Ham

GLAZED HAM

1 (8-pound) smoked Virginia ham (shank end)
½ cup peach preserves
1 tablespoon coarse-grained mustard
¾ teaspoon TABASCO® brand Pepper Sauce
⅛ teaspoon ground cloves

PEACH-CORN PICCALILLI

3 large ripe peaches
1 tablespoon vegetable oil
1 medium red bell pepper, seeded and diced
¼ cup sliced green onions
1 (17-ounce) can corn, drained
2 tablespoons brown sugar
2 tablespoons cider vinegar
1 teaspoon TABASCO® brand Pepper Sauce
¼ teaspoon salt

Heat oven to 325°F. Remove skin from ham; trim off any excess fat. Score fat ¼ inch deep in 1-inch diamonds. Place ham, fat side up, in roasting pan. Insert ovenproof meat thermometer into thickest part of ham, not touching the bone. Bake 1½ hours until thermometer reaches 135°F.

Meanwhile, prepare glaze. Mix peach preserves, mustard, TABASCO® Sauce and cloves in small bowl. Remove ham from oven, maintaining oven temperature; brush with peach glaze. Bake 20 minutes longer or until the temperature reaches 160°F.

Meanwhile, prepare Peach-Corn Piccalilli. Peel and cut peaches in half and remove pits. Chop two of the peach halves; set aside. Heat oil in 2-quart saucepan over medium heat. Add red pepper and green onions. Cook 3 minutes, stirring frequently. Add corn, brown sugar, vinegar, TABASCO® Sauce and salt. Heat to boiling; stir in chopped peaches. Reduce heat to low; cover and simmer 5 minutes or until peaches are just tender. To serve, arrange ham on a large platter. Fill remaining peach halves with Peach-Corn Piccalilli and arrange around ham on platter. *Makes 8 to 12 servings*

Country Captain Chicken

4 boneless skinless chicken thighs
2 tablespoons all-purpose flour
2 tablespoons vegetable oil, divided
1 cup chopped green bell pepper
1 large onion, chopped
1 rib celery, chopped
1 clove garlic, minced
¼ cup chicken broth
2 cups canned crushed tomatoes or diced fresh tomatoes
½ cup golden raisins
1½ teaspoons curry powder
1 teaspoon salt
¼ teaspoon paprika
¼ teaspoon black pepper
2 cups hot cooked rice

SLOW COOKER DIRECTIONS

1. Coat chicken with flour; set aside. Heat 1 tablespoon oil in large skillet over medium-high heat until hot. Add bell pepper, onion, celery and garlic. Cook and stir 5 minutes or until vegetables are tender. Place vegetables in slow cooker.

2. Heat remaining 1 tablespoon oil in same skillet over medium-high heat. Add chicken; cook 5 minutes per side or until browned. Place chicken in slow cooker.

3. Pour broth into skillet. Heat over medium-high heat, stirring frequently and scraping up any browned bits from bottom of skillet. Pour liquid into slow cooker. Add tomatoes, raisins, curry powder, salt, paprika and black pepper. Cover; cook on LOW 3 hours. Serve chicken with sauce over rice.

Makes 4 servings

Carolina Barbecue

1 (5-pound) pork Boston butt roast
2 teaspoons vegetable oil
1½ cups water
1 can (8 ounces) tomato sauce
¼ cup packed brown sugar
¼ cup cider vinegar
¼ cup Worcestershire sauce
1 teaspoon celery seeds
1 teaspoon chili powder
Salt and black pepper to taste
Dash hot pepper sauce

Randomly pierce roast with sharp knife. In Dutch oven, brown roast on all sides in hot oil. In mixing bowl, combine remaining ingredients; mix well. Pour sauce over roast and bring to a boil. Reduce heat; cover and simmer 2 hours or until roast is fork-tender. Baste roast with sauce during cooking time. Slice or chop to serve. *Makes 20 servings*

Favorite recipe from **National Pork Board**

Chicken Étouffée

Dry Roux (page 109)
4 chicken breasts
¾ teaspoon salt
½ teaspoon ground red pepper
¼ teaspoon black pepper
1 tablespoon vegetable oil
3 cups chopped yellow onions
½ cup chopped green bell pepper
1 cup water, divided
3 large cloves garlic, minced
3 cups chicken broth
¼ cup chopped green onions

1. Prepare Dry Roux.

2. Remove skin and fat from chicken. Combine salt, ground red pepper and black pepper in cup; sprinkle 1 teaspoon mixture over chicken. Heat oil in large heavy skillet over medium heat. Add chicken; cover and cook about 20 minutes or until browned on all sides, draining any liquid in pan halfway through cooking time.

3. Remove chicken from skillet. Add yellow onions and bell pepper; cover and cook 10 to 15 minutes or until onions begin to brown, stirring occasionally. Add ⅓ cup water and increase heat to medium-high. Cook about 10 minutes or until mixture begins to stick and brown again, stirring frequently and watching carefully to prevent burning. Add ⅓ cup water; cook and stir until mixture begins to stick and brown again. Add remaining ⅓ cup water and garlic; cook until mixture begins to stick and brown again, stirring frequently.

4. Stir in chicken broth; bring to a boil over medium-high heat. Quickly whisk in Dry Roux until smooth and well mixed; cook 5 minutes. Add chicken and remaining ½ teaspoon salt mixture to skillet; bring to a boil.

5. Reduce heat to medium-low; simmer about 15 minutes or until mixture is thickened and chicken is no longer pink in center. Sprinkle with green onions. Serve over rice. Garnish with green bell pepper and carrot, if desired.

Makes 4 servings

DRY ROUX: Heat medium nonstick skillet over medium-high heat about 3 minutes. Add ⅓ cup flour to skillet; cook 10 to 15 minutes or until flour turns the color of peanut butter or light cinnamon, stirring frequently to prevent burning. Sift flour into small bowl; set aside.

Savory Chicken and Biscuits

1 pound boneless, skinless chicken thighs or breasts,
    cut into 1-inch pieces

1 medium potato, cut into 1-inch pieces

1 medium yellow onion, cut into 1-inch pieces

8 ounces fresh mushrooms, quartered

1 cup fresh baby carrots

1 cup chopped celery

1 (14½-ounce) can chicken broth

3 cloves garlic, minced

1 teaspoon dried rosemary leaves

1 teaspoon salt

1 teaspoon black pepper

3 tablespoons cornstarch blended with ½ cup cold water

1 cup frozen peas, thawed

1 (4-ounce) jar sliced pimientos, drained

1 package BOB EVANS® Frozen Buttermilk Biscuit Dough

Preheat oven to 375°F. Combine chicken, potato, onion, mushrooms, carrots, celery, broth, garlic, rosemary, salt and pepper in large saucepan. Bring to a boil over high heat. Reduce heat to low and simmer, uncovered, 5 minutes. Stir in cornstarch mixture; cook 2 minutes. Stir in peas and pimientos; return to a boil. Transfer chicken mixture to 2-quart casserole dish; arrange frozen biscuits on top. Bake 30 to 35 minutes or until biscuits are golden brown. Refrigerate leftovers.   *Makes 4 to 6 servings*

Savory Chicken and Biscuits

COASTAL
Fish & Seafood

Magic Fried Oysters

6 dozen medium to large shucked oysters in their liquor
  (about 3 pounds)
3 tablespoons Chef Paul Prudhomme's Seafood Magic®
1 cup all-purpose flour
1 cup corn flour
1 cup cornmeal
  Vegetable oil for deep-frying

Place oysters and oyster liquor in large bowl. Add 2 tablespoons of the
Seafood Magic® to oysters, stirring well. In medium bowl, combine flour,
corn flour, cornmeal and the remaining 1 tablespoon Seafood Magic®. Heat
2 inches or more of oil in deep-fryer or large saucepan to 375°F. Drain
oysters and then use a slotted spoon to toss them lightly and quickly in
seasoned flour mixture (so oysters don't produce excess moisture, which
cakes the flour); shake off excess flour and carefully slip each oyster into hot
oil. Fry in single layer in batches just until crispy and golden brown, 1 to
1½ minutes; do not overcook. (Adjust heat as needed to maintain
temperature at about 375°F.) Drain on paper towels and serve.

Makes 6 servings

Magic Fried Oysters

Blackened Snapper with Red Onion Salsa

Cajun Seasoning Mix (recipe follows)
Red Onion Salsa (page 115)
4 red snapper fillets (about 6 ounces each)
2 tablespoons butter

Prepare Cajun Seasoning Mix and Red Onion Salsa; set aside. Rinse red snapper and pat dry with paper towels. Sprinkle both sides of each fillet with 1 tablespoon Cajun Seasoning Mix. Heat large, heavy skillet over high heat until very hot. Add butter and swirl skillet to coat bottom. When butter no longer bubbles, place fish in pan. Cook fish 6 to 8 minutes or until surface is very brown and fish flakes easily when tested with fork, turning halfway through cooking. Serve with Red Onion Salsa. ***Makes 4 servings***

Cajun Seasoning Mix

2 tablespoons salt
1 tablespoon paprika
1½ teaspoons garlic powder
1 teaspoon onion powder
1 teaspoon ground red pepper
½ teaspoon white pepper
½ teaspoon black pepper
½ teaspoon dried thyme leaves
½ teaspoon dried oregano leaves

Combine all ingredients in small bowl. ***Makes about ½ cup***

Red Onion Salsa

1 tablespoon vegetable oil
1 large red onion, chopped
1 clove garlic, minced
½ cup chicken broth
¼ cup dry red wine or red wine vinegar
¼ teaspoon dried thyme leaves
Salt and black pepper to taste

Heat oil in small saucepan over medium-high heat. Add onion; cover and cook 5 minutes. Add garlic; cook 1 minute. Add remaining ingredients. Cover; cook about 10 minutes. Uncover; cook until liquid reduces to ¼ cup.

Makes about 1 cup

Fresh Corn Relish

¼ cup cooked fresh corn or thawed frozen corn
¼ cup finely diced green bell pepper
¼ cup finely slivered red onion
1 tablespoon vegetable oil
2 tablespoons seasoned (sweet) rice vinegar
Salt and black pepper
½ cup cherry tomatoes, cut into quarters

Toss together corn, green pepper, onion, oil and vinegar in medium bowl. Season with salt and pepper. Cover; refrigerate until ready to serve. Just before serving, gently mix in tomatoes. *Makes about 1½ cups*

Catfish with Fresh Corn Relish

4 catfish fillets (each about 6 ounces and at least ½ inch thick)
2 tablespoons paprika
½ teaspoon ground red pepper
½ teaspoon salt
   Fresh Corn Relish (page 115)
   Lime wedges
   Grilled baking potatoes (optional)
   Tarragon sprigs for garnish

Rinse fish; pat dry with paper towels. Combine paprika, red pepper and salt in cup; lightly sprinkle on both sides of fish.

Oil hot grid to help prevent sticking. Grill fish, on a covered grill, over medium KINGSFORD® Briquets, 5 to 9 minutes. Halfway through cooking time, turn fish over and continue grilling until fish turns from translucent to opaque throughout. (Grilling time depends on the thickness of fish; allow 3 to 5 minutes for each ½ inch of thickness.) Serve with Fresh Corn Relish, lime wedges and potatoes, if desired. Garnish with tarragon sprigs.

Makes 4 servings

Because fish cooks quickly, watch it closely while grilling. When the fish is done, it feels slightly springy, looks opaque and has lost all shininess. Don't wait until it flakes easily or the fish will be dry.

Catfish with Fresh Corn Relish

Oyster Po' Boys

Spicy Mayonnaise (recipe follows)
¾ cup cornmeal
¼ cup all-purpose flour
½ teaspoon salt
⅛ teaspoon black pepper
¾ cup oil for frying
2 pints shucked oysters, drained
4 French bread rolls,* split
Lettuce leaves
Tomato slices

Or, substitute French bread loaf, split and cut into 4-inch lengths, for French bread rolls.

1. Prepare Spicy Mayonnaise; cover and set aside.

2. Combine cornmeal, flour, salt and pepper in shallow bowl; set aside.

3. Heat oil in medium skillet over medium heat. Pat oysters dry with paper towels. Dip oysters in cornmeal mixture to coat.

4. Fry in batches 5 minutes or until golden brown, turning once. Drain on paper towels.

5. Spread rolls with Spicy Mayonnaise; fill with lettuce, tomatoes and oysters.   *Makes 4 sandwiches*

Spicy Mayonnaise

½ cup mayonnaise
2 tablespoons plain yogurt
1 clove garlic, minced
¼ teaspoon ground red pepper

Combine all ingredients in small bowl; mix until well blended.

Makes ½ cup

Oyster Po' Boy

Crawfish (Seafood) Boil

1 gallon water
2 (3-ounce) packages crab boil
⅓ cup salt
¼ cup TABASCO® brand Pepper Sauce
1 large lemon, cut into quarters
8 medium white onions, peeled
4 artichokes, cut into halves
3 carrots, peeled and cut into 2-inch pieces
1½ pounds small red potatoes
4 ears corn, cut into 3-inch pieces
3 pounds crawfish*
1 pound large shrimp, unpeeled
1 pound andouille sausage or kielbasa, cut into 2-inch pieces

*Or, substitute other shellfish for crawfish. Cook blue crabs 20 minutes, lobsters 25 minutes per pound or Dungeness crabs 25 to 30 minutes.

Heat water, crab boil, salt, TABASCO® Sauce and lemon to boiling in very large pot with removable wire basket. Add onions, artichokes, carrots and potatoes; heat to boiling. Reduce heat to low; cover and simmer 20 minutes or until vegetables are tender. Carefully remove vegetables from pot; keep warm.

Add corn, crawfish, shrimp and sausage to boiling mixture; bring to a boil over high heat. Reduce heat to low; cover and simmer 5 to 8 minutes or until crawfish and shrimp are pink and corn is tender. Carefully remove corn, seafood and sausage.

To serve, arrange vegetables, seafood and sausage on large platter or place on newspaper or brown paper. Serve with cold beer and French bread.

Makes 8 servings

NOTE: Crab boil, also called shrimp boil, is a blend of herbs and spices found in the spice section of supermarkets and specialty stores.

Devilishly Stuffed Soft-Shell Crab

8 soft-shell Florida blue crabs, cleaned, fresh or frozen
¼ cup chopped onion
¼ cup chopped celery
2 tablespoons chopped green bell pepper
1 clove garlic, minced
¼ cup margarine or butter, melted
1 cup buttery cracker crumbs
2 tablespoons milk
1 egg, beaten
1 tablespoon chopped parsley
½ teaspoon dry mustard
½ teaspoon Worcestershire sauce
¼ teaspoon salt
⅛ teaspoon cayenne pepper
¼ cup margarine or butter, melted

Thaw crabs if frozen. Wash crabs thoroughly; drain well. Cook onion, celery, green pepper and garlic in ¼ cup margarine until tender. In medium bowl, combine onion mixture, cracker crumbs, milk, egg, parsley, mustard, Worcestershire sauce, salt and cayenne pepper. Place crabs in shallow, well-greased baking pan. Remove top shell from crabs and fill each cavity with 1 tablespoon stuffing mixture. Replace top shell. Brush crabs with ¼ cup melted margarine. Bake in preheated 400°F oven 15 minutes or until shells turn red and crabs brown slightly. **_Makes 4 servings_**

Favorite recipe from **Florida Department of Agriculture and Consumer Services, Bureau of Seafood and Aquaculture**

Cajun Catfish with Red Beans and Rice

Red Beans and Rice (page 124)
6 skinless catfish fillets (6 ounces each)
12 frozen, deveined, shelled large shrimp, thawed
⅓ cup olive oil
1 teaspoon dried thyme leaves
1 teaspoon dried oregano leaves
2 cloves garlic, minced
½ teaspoon salt
½ teaspoon black pepper
⅛ to ¼ teaspoon ground red pepper
6 sheets (15×12 inches) heavy-duty foil, lightly sprayed
    with nonstick cooking spray

1. Preheat oven to 450°F. Prepare Red Beans and Rice, if desired.

2. Place catfish and shrimp in resealable plastic food storage bag. Combine oil, thyme, oregano, garlic, salt, black pepper and red pepper in small bowl. Add to bag. Seal bag; turn bag to coat fish and shrimp. Marinate 30 minutes.

3. Remove fish and shrimp from marinade; discard remaining marinade. Place one fish fillet in center of 1 foil sheet. Top with 2 shrimp.

4. Double fold sides and ends of foil to seal packet, leaving head space for heat circulation. Repeat with remaining fish, shrimp and foil sheets to make 5 more packets. Place packets on baking sheet.

5. Bake 25 minutes. Let stand 5 minutes. Open packet and transfer contents to serving plates. Serve with Red Beans and Rice.   ***Makes 6 servings***

Cajun Catfish with Red Beans and Rice

Red Beans and Rice

1 cup water
½ cup uncooked rice
½ teaspoon salt
1 can (15 ounces) kidney beans, rinsed and drained
1 can (14½ ounces) diced tomatoes, undrained
2 tablespoons bacon bits
1 tablespoon chili powder
1 large heavy-duty foil baking bag (17×15 inches), lightly sprayed
   with nonstick cooking spray

1. Preheat oven to 450°F.

2. Place water, rice and salt in 2-quart microwavable container; microwave at HIGH 7 minutes.

3. Add remaining ingredients, except foil bag; stir until blended. Place foil bag in 1-inch deep jelly-roll pan; spoon rice mixture into bag. Double fold bag to seal. Shake baking pan to distribute contents of bag evenly.

4. Bake 45 minutes. Let stand 5 minutes. Carefully cut bag open. Fold back top to allow steam to escape.   ***Makes 6 (1-cup) servings***

NOTE: For a milder flavor, reduce chili powder to 2 teaspoons.

Southern Fried Catfish with Hush Puppies

Hush Puppy Batter (recipe follows)
4 catfish fillets (about 1½ pounds)
½ cup yellow cornmeal
3 tablespoons all-purpose flour
1½ teaspoons salt
¼ teaspoon ground red pepper

1. Prepare Hush Puppy Batter; set aside.

2. Rinse catfish; pat dry with paper towels. Combine cornmeal, flour, salt and red pepper in shallow dish. Dip fish in cornmeal mixture. Heat 1 inch vegetable oil in large, heavy saucepan over medium heat until oil registers 375°F on deep-fry thermometer.

3. Fry fish, a few pieces at a time, 4 to 5 minutes or until golden brown and fish flakes easily. Allow temperature of oil to return to 375°F between each batch. Drain fish on paper towels.

4. To make Hush Puppies, drop batter by tablespoonfuls into hot oil. Fry, a few pieces at a time, 2 minutes or until golden brown.

Makes 4 servings

Hush Puppy Batter

1½ cups yellow cornmeal
½ cup all-purpose flour
2 teaspoons baking powder
½ teaspoon salt
1 cup milk
1 small onion, minced
1 egg, lightly beaten

Combine cornmeal, flour, baking powder and salt in medium bowl. Add milk, onion and egg. Stir until well blended. Allow batter to stand 5 to 10 minutes before frying. ***Makes about 24 hush puppies***

Steamed Maryland Crabs

2 cups water or beer
2 cups cider vinegar or white vinegar
2 dozen live Maryland blue crabs
½ pound seafood seasoning
½ pound salt

1. Place water and vinegar in 10-gallon stockpot. Place rack in bottom of pot. Place half of crabs on rack. Mix seafood seasoning with salt; sprinkle half over crabs.

2. Repeat layering with remaining crabs and seasoning mixture.

3. Cover pot. Cook over high heat until liquid begins to steam. Steam about 25 minutes or until crabs turn red and meat is white. Remove crabs to large serving platter using tongs.

4. Cover table with disposable paper cloth.

5. To pick crabs, place crab on its back. With thumb or knife point, pry off "apron" flap (the "pull tab" looking shell in the center) and discard.

6. Lift off top shell and discard.

7. Break off toothed claws and set aside. With knife edge, scrape off 3 areas of lungs and debris over hard semi-transparent membrane covering edible crabmeat.

8. Hold crab at each side; break apart at center. Discard legs. Remove membrane cover with knife, exposing large chunks of meat; remove with fingers or knife.

9. Crack claws with mallet or knife handle to expose meat.

Makes 4 servings

Steamed Maryland Crabs

Blazing Catfish Po' Boys

1½ **pounds catfish fillets**
¾ **cup yellow cornmeal**
1 **egg**
⅓ **cup *Frank's® RedHot® *Original Cayenne Pepper Sauce**
6 **sandwich rolls, split in half**
    Spicy Tartar Sauce (recipe follows)
3 **cups deli coleslaw**

1. Cut fillets crosswise into 1-inch-wide strips. Combine cornmeal and *½ teaspoon salt* on sheet of waxed paper. Beat egg with *Frank's RedHot* Sauce in medium bowl. Dip fish pieces in egg mixture; shake off excess. Thoroughly coat with cornmeal mixture.

2. Heat *1½ cups vegetable oil* in large deep skillet or electric fryer until hot (360°F). Cook fish, in batches, 5 minutes or until cooked through and golden on all sides, turning once. Drain on paper towels.

3. Hollow out rolls if necessary. Spread bottom of each roll with about *2 tablespoons* Spicy Tartar Sauce. Layer with *½ cup* coleslaw and a few pieces of fish. Cover with top of roll.   ***Makes 6 sandwiches***

SPICY TARTAR SAUCE: Combine ⅔ cup prepared tartar sauce with ¼ cup *Frank's RedHot* Sauce.

PREP TIME: 15 minutes
COOK TIME: 5 minutes

Blazing Catfish Po' Boy

DOWN HOME
Sides & Salads

Apple Buttered Sweet Potatoes

1 pound sweet potatoes, cooked, peeled and sliced
1 cup (11-ounce jar) SMUCKER'S® Cider Apple Butter
⅓ cup SMUCKER'S® Pineapple Topping
2 tablespoons butter or margarine, melted
½ teaspoon salt
¼ teaspoon ground cinnamon
¼ teaspoon paprika

Arrange sliced sweet potatoes in ungreased shallow baking dish. Combine apple butter and remaining ingredients; mix well. Drizzle mixture over sweet potatoes.

Bake at 350°F for 20 to 30 minutes or until heated through.

Makes 6 servings

Apple Buttered Sweet Potatoes

Creamy Coleslaw

½ **medium head cabbage, outer leaves removed and cut in half**
¼ **cup mayonnaise**
2 **tablespoons cider vinegar**
1 **tablespoon plus 1½ teaspoons sugar**
¼ **teaspoon salt**
    Black pepper

1. Cut core from cabbage quarters; coarsely shred cabbage into medium bowl using box grater.

2. Combine mayonnaise, vinegar, sugar, salt and pepper in small bowl; mix well. Pour over cabbage; stir until well blended. Cover and refrigerate at least 2 hours or overnight.   *Makes 4 to 6 servings*

Classic Macaroni and Cheese

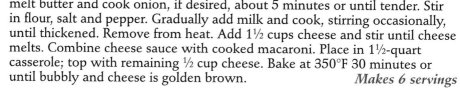

2 **cups elbow macaroni**
3 **tablespoons butter or margarine**
¼ **cup chopped onion (optional)**
2 **tablespoons all-purpose flour**
½ **teaspoon salt**
⅛ **teaspoon pepper**
2 **cups milk**
2 **cups (8 ounces) SARGENTO® Chef Style**
    or Fancy Mild Cheddar Shredded Cheese, divided

Cook macaroni according to package directions; drain. In medium saucepan, melt butter and cook onion, if desired, about 5 minutes or until tender. Stir in flour, salt and pepper. Gradually add milk and cook, stirring occasionally, until thickened. Remove from heat. Add 1½ cups cheese and stir until cheese melts. Combine cheese sauce with cooked macaroni. Place in 1½-quart casserole; top with remaining ½ cup cheese. Bake at 350°F 30 minutes or until bubbly and cheese is golden brown.   *Makes 6 servings*

Traditional Potato Salad

2 tablespoons plus 1 teaspoon Chef Paul Prudhomme's
    Vegetable Magic®
1 teaspoon salt
1½ cups salad dressing or mayonnaise
4 medium-size white potatoes, cooked, peeled and diced
    into ½-inch cubes
6 hard-boiled eggs, peeled and finely chopped
¼ cup finely diced onions
¼ cup finely diced celery
¼ cup finely diced green bell peppers

Blend the Vegetable Magic and salt into the salad dressing or mayonnaise in
a large bowl, then add all the remaining ingredients. Mix well and refrigerate
until ready to serve.   *Makes 6 to 8 side-dish servings*

Microwaved Vidalia Onion

1 large Vidalia or other sweet onion
1 beef, chicken or vegetable bouillon cube
1 teaspoon butter

1. Peel outer skin from onion. Cut slice off bottom root end of onion so it
stands upright. Cut cone shape out of top of onion with small sharp knife,
leaving at least ½ inch intact in bottom of onion.

2. Place onion in bowl. Place bouillon cube and butter in hole in onion. Fill
bowl with water, covering onion halfway up side. Cover onion and bowl
loosely with waxed paper; microwave at HIGH 5 to 6 minutes or until onion
is tender and can be separated with fork. Serve broth with onion.

Makes 1 serving

Southern-Style Succotash

2 tablespoons butter
1 cup chopped onion
1 package (10 ounces) frozen lima beans, thawed
1 cup frozen whole corn kernels, thawed
½ cup chopped red bell pepper
1 can (15 to 16 ounces) hominy, drained
⅓ cup chicken broth
½ teaspoon salt
¼ teaspoon hot pepper sauce
¼ cup chopped green onion tops or chives

1. Melt butter in large nonstick skillet over medium heat. Add onion; cook and stir 5 minutes. Add lima beans, corn and bell pepper. Cook and stir 5 minutes.

2. Add hominy, chicken broth, salt and pepper sauce; simmer 5 minutes or until most of liquid has evaporated. Remove from heat; stir in green onion tops.

Makes 6 servings

Magic Broiled Tomatoes

2 medium-sized tomatoes, peeled
1 tablespoon plus 1 teaspoon unsalted butter, softened
2 teaspoons Chef Paul Prudhomme's Vegetable Magic®
1 tablespoon grated Parmesan cheese (optional)

Preheat the broiler. Score the tomatoes about 4 times across the top to about half-way down; set aside. Make a paste of the butter, the Vegetable Magic and the Parmesan, if desired. Spread half the mixture on top of each tomato pushing a little mixture down into the scoring. Place the tomatoes in a shallow pan, seasoned side up. Broil with tomato tops about 1 inch from heat until tops are brown and crusty, about 3 minutes. Serve immediately with any juices from the bottom of the pan spooned over the top.

Makes 2 servings

Southern Collard Greens

2 bunches collard greens
1 small ham hock
¼ cup apple cider vinegar
¼ cup olive oil
1 small onion, quartered
3 cloves garlic, halved
1 can (about 14 ounces) chicken broth
1 cup water
2 tablespoons butter
Pinch *each* of sugar, salt and black pepper

1. Wash greens well. Remove and discard stems; coarsely chop leaves. Cover; set aside.

2. Rinse ham hock; place in Dutch oven. Cover with water; add vinegar. Bring to a boil; reduce heat and simmer 20 minutes. Remove ham hock from Dutch oven; discard liquid.

3. Heat oil in same pan over medium heat until hot. Cook and stir onion and garlic until onion is translucent. Add ham hock, greens, broth and water. Cover; cook over medium heat 1 hour 15 minutes or until greens are tender, stirring occasionally. Add additional broth or water if needed. Add butter, sugar, salt and pepper; stir until butter melts. *Makes 4 to 5 servings*

When purchasing collard greens, one pound fresh greens makes about 3 cups cooked greens. Store greens in plastic bags for up to 5 days in the refrigerator. When ready to prepare, remove any tough stems by folding each leaf in half. Pull the stem toward the top of the leaf. Then, follow the instructions in the recipe.

Bayou Dirty Rice

¼ **pound spicy sausage, crumbled**
½ **medium onion, chopped**
1 **stalk celery, sliced**
1 **package (6 ounces) wild and long grain rice seasoned mix**
1 **can (14½ ounces) DEL MONTE® Stewed Tomatoes - Original Recipe**
½ **green bell pepper, chopped**
¼ **cup chopped parsley**

1. Brown sausage and onion in large skillet over medium-high heat; drain. Add celery, rice and rice seasoning packet; cook and stir 2 minutes.

2. Drain tomatoes, reserving liquid; pour liquid into measuring cup. Add water to measure 1⅓ cups; pour over rice. Add tomatoes; bring to boil. Cover and cook over low heat 20 minutes. Add bell pepper and parsley.

3. Cover and cook 5 minutes or until rice is tender.

Makes 4 to 6 servings

PREP & COOK TIME: 40 minutes

Southern Ham and Pea Salad

2 **cups frozen peas, thawed and drained**
1 **cup (6 ounces) diced CURE 81® ham**
½ **cup thinly sliced red bell pepper**
½ **cup prepared poppy seed salad dressing**
¼ **cup sliced green onion**
⅔ **cup chopped pecans, toasted**
   Boston lettuce leaves

In large bowl, combine peas, ham, bell pepper, dressing and green onion; stir well. Cover and refrigerate at least 1 hour. To serve, stir in pecans. Arrange lettuce leaves on individual serving plates. Spoon salad mixture evenly into lettuce cups.

Makes 4 servings

Bayou Dirty Rice

Summer Squash Casserole

2 cups sliced yellow summer squash
1 medium carrot, thinly sliced
½ cup chopped onion
½ cup diced red or green bell pepper
½ teaspoon salt
⅛ teaspoon black pepper
1 can (10¾ ounces) condensed cream of chicken
  or mushroom soup, undiluted
1 container (8 ounces) sour cream
1 cup (4 ounces) shredded Italian cheese blend
1 cup (4 ounces) shredded Cheddar cheese
1 package (6 ounces) stuffing mix

1. Preheat oven to 350°F. Combine squash, carrot, onion, bell pepper, salt and black pepper in medium saucepan; cover with water. Bring to a boil; cook 5 minutes or until tender; drain.

2. Combine soup and sour cream in 13×9-inch casserole; mix well. Stir in vegetable mixture; spread evenly. Sprinkle cheeses on top. Top with stuffing mix. Bake, covered, 30 minutes. *Makes 6 servings*

Red Rice

2 cups chicken broth, beef broth or water
1 cup uncooked long-grain rice
2 tablespoons tomato sauce *or* 2 teaspoons tomato paste
1 tablespoon FILIPPO BERIO® Olive Oil
  Salt and freshly ground black pepper

In 3-quart saucepan, combine chicken broth, rice, tomato sauce and olive oil. Bring to a boil over medium-high heat; stir once. Cover; reduce heat to low and simmer 15 minutes or until rice is tender and liquid is absorbed. Remove from heat; let stand, covered, 5 to 10 minutes. Season to taste with salt and pepper. *Makes 4 to 6 servings*

Spicy Greens with Smoked Turkey

  1 large onion, chopped
  3 cloves garlic, minced
1½ pounds smoked turkey wings, cut at joints
  4 pounds young collard greens (about 4 bunches)
  ¼ cup *Frank's® RedHot®* Original Cayenne Pepper Sauce
  1 tablespoon brown sugar

1. Heat *1 tablespoon oil* in 8-quart saucepot. Cook and stir onion and garlic 3 minutes or until just tender. Add turkey wings and *2 cups water* to saucepot. Heat to boiling. Reduce heat to medium-low. Cook, covered, 10 minutes. Set aside.

2. Pick through greens, discarding yellow leaves and thick stems. Rinse thoroughly in several changes of water to remove all grit. Stack several leaves together. Slice lengthwise through center of stack; then crosswise into 1-inch wide strips. Repeat with remaining leaves. Gradually add greens to saucepot, stirring often over medium-low heat from bottom of pot as greens cook down. Cook, partially covered, 45 minutes or until just tender. Stir occasionally.

3. Stir in *Frank's RedHot* Sauce and sugar. Cook, partially covered, over medium-low heat 15 minutes or until greens are of desired tenderness. Stir occasionally. Remove from heat. Transfer wings to plate; cool slightly. Cut meat from bones; shred into pieces. Stir into greens. To serve, spoon greens into bowls with flavorful "potlikker." Serve with cornbread, if desired.

Makes 6 servings

PREP TIME: 30 minutes
COOK TIME: 70 minutes

Fried Green Tomatoes

2 medium green tomatoes
¼ cup all-purpose flour
¼ cup yellow cornmeal
½ teaspoon salt
½ teaspoon garlic salt
½ teaspoon ground red pepper
½ teaspoon cracked black pepper
1 cup buttermilk
1 cup vegetable oil
Hot pepper sauce (optional)

1. Cut tomatoes into ¼-inch-thick slices. Combine flour, cornmeal, salt, garlic salt, red pepper and black pepper in pie plate or shallow bowl; mix well. Pour buttermilk into second pie plate or shallow bowl.

2. Heat oil in large skillet over medium heat. Meanwhile, dip tomato slices into buttermilk, coating both sides. Immediately dredge slices in flour mixture; shake off excess flour mixture.

3. Cook tomato slices in hot oil 3 to 5 minutes per side. Transfer to parchment paper or paper towels. Serve immediately with pepper sauce, if desired. **Makes 3 to 4 servings**

SERVING SUGGESTION: Serve fried green tomatoes with shredded lettuce.

Fried Green Tomatoes

Gourmet Grits

½ pound **BOB EVANS®** Italian Roll Sausage
 3 cups water
 1 cup uncooked white grits
½ (10-ounce) package frozen chopped spinach, thawed and
  squeezed dry
¼ cup grated Parmesan cheese
¼ cup chopped sun-dried tomatoes
¼ cup olive oil
 1 clove garlic, chopped

Crumble sausage into medium skillet. Cook over medium heat until browned, stirring occasionally. Drain off any drippings; set aside. Bring water to a rapid boil in large saucepan. While stirring, add grits in steady stream until mixture thickens into smooth paste. Reduce heat to low; simmer 5 to 7 minutes, stirring frequently to prevent sticking. Stir in sausage, spinach, cheese and tomatoes. Pour into greased 9×5-inch loaf pan. Refrigerate until cool and firm.

Unmold. Slice into ½-inch-thick slices. Heat oil in large skillet over medium-high heat until hot. Add garlic; cook and stir 30 seconds or until soft. Add grit slices, 4 to 5 at a time, and cook until golden brown on both sides. Repeat until all slices are cooked. Serve hot. Refrigerate leftovers.

Makes 4 to 6 side-dish servings

SERVING SUGGESTION: Melt thin slice of mozzarella cheese on top of each browned slice. This also makes a wonderful side dish for chicken, topped with warmed seasoned tomato or spaghetti sauce.

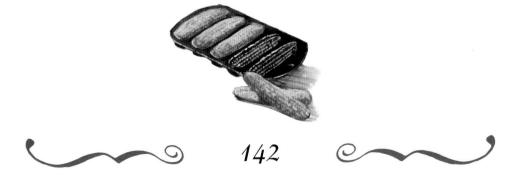

Hoppin' John Skillet

1 (7.2-ounce) package RICE-A-RONI® Rice Pilaf
1 small onion, chopped
2 cloves garlic, minced
2 tablespoons margarine or butter
1½ cups fresh or frozen cut green beans or sliced fresh okra
1 (15-ounce) can black-eyed peas, rinsed and drained
¾ teaspoon hot pepper sauce
1 small tomato, chopped

1. In large skillet over medium heat, sauté rice-pasta mix, onion and garlic with margarine until pasta is light golden brown.

2. Slowly stir in 2 cups water, green beans and Special Seasonings; bring to a boil. Cover; reduce heat to low. Simmer 10 minutes.

3. Stir in black-eyed peas and hot pepper sauce. Cover; simmer 10 to 12 minutes or until rice is tender. Stir in tomato. Let stand 3 minutes.

Makes 4 servings

PREP TIME: 5 minutes
COOK TIME: 25 minutes

Southern Secret

Hoppin' John is a flavorful dish that combines black-eyed peas, onion and rice in a satisfying, simmered pilaf. It has been a Southern tradition to serve black-eyed peas on new Year's Day. They are said to bring good luck and prosperity for the new year.

Deviled Eggs

12 large eggs, at room temperature
1 tablespoon vinegar
   Lettuce leaves

FILLING

   3 tablespoons *Frank's® RedHot®* Original Cayenne Pepper Sauce
   2 tablespoons mayonnaise
   2 tablespoons sour cream
   ½ cup minced celery
   ¼ cup minced red onion
   ¼ teaspoon garlic powder

1. Place eggs in a single layer in bottom of large saucepan; cover with water. Add vinegar to water. Bring to a full boil. Immediately remove from heat. Cover; let stand 15 minutes. Drain eggs and rinse with cold water. Set eggs in bowl of ice water; cool.

2. To peel eggs, tap against side of counter. Gently remove shells, holding eggs under running water. Slice eggs in half lengthwise; remove yolks to medium bowl. Arrange whites on lettuce-lined platter.

3. To make Filling, add *Frank's RedHot* Sauce, mayonnaise and sour cream to egg yolks in bowl. Mix until well blended and creamy. Stir in celery, onion and garlic powder; mix well. Spoon about 1 tablespoon filling into each egg white. Garnish with parsley, capers or caviar, if desired. Cover with plastic wrap; refrigerate 30 minutes before serving.

Makes 12 servings (about 1½ cups filling)

TIP: Filling may be piped into whites through large star-shaped pastry tip inserted into corner of plastic bag.

PREP TIME: 40 minutes
COOK TIME: 20 minutes
CHILL TIME: 30 minutes

Black-Eyed Peas

1 bag (1 pound) dried black-eyed peas, soaked overnight, drained
1½ cups diced onion
2 shallots, finely chopped
⅓ green bell pepper, cored, seeded and chopped
¼ cup vegetable oil
1 teaspoon salt
1 teaspoon black pepper
3 to 4 cups water

1. Place soaked black-eyed peas in large stockpot. Add onion, shallots and bell pepper. Cover; let stand about 20 minutes for peas to absorb flavors.

2. Add oil, salt and pepper; stir. Cover; let stand an additional 10 to 15 minutes for peas to absorb flavor.

3. Add 3 to 4 cups of water, to cover the peas by a depth of 1 inch. Bring to a boil; lower heat and simmer, covered, 50 to 60 minutes or until tender.

4. Before serving, remove ½ cup cooked peas. Mash and stir back into the pot to thicken the cooking liquid.   ***Makes 10 servings***

NOTE: Black-eyed peas are small tan beans named for the black eye-shaped mark on the inner curve of the bean. Long, slow cooking with ham or salt pork enhances their mealy texture and earthy flavor. These beans are occasionally available fresh, but for the most part, they are dried or canned.

 145

Sweet Potato Gratin

    3 pounds sweet potatoes (about 5 large)
    ½ cup (1 stick) butter, divided
    ¼ cup plus 2 tablespoons packed light brown sugar, divided
    2 eggs
    ⅔ cup orange juice
    2 teaspoons ground cinnamon, divided
    ½ teaspoon salt
    ¼ teaspoon ground nutmeg
    ⅓ cup all-purpose flour
    ¼ cup uncooked old-fashioned oats
    ⅓ cup chopped pecans or walnuts

1. Preheat oven to 350°F. Bake sweet potatoes about 1 hour or until tender. Or, pierce sweet potatoes several times with fork and place on microwavable plate. Microwave at HIGH 16 to 18 minutes, rotating and turning over potatoes after 9 minutes. Let stand 5 minutes.

2. Cut hot sweet potatoes lengthwise into halves. Scrape hot pulp from skins into large bowl.

3. Beat ¼ cup butter and 2 tablespoons sugar into sweet potatoes with electric mixer at medium speed until butter is melted. Add eggs, orange juice, 1½ teaspoons cinnamon, salt and nutmeg. Beat until smooth. Pour mixture into 1½-quart baking dish or gratin dish; smooth top.

4. For topping, combine flour, oats, remaining ¼ cup sugar and remaining ½ teaspoon cinnamon in medium bowl. Cut in remaining ¼ cup butter until mixture resembles coarse crumbs. Stir in pecans. Sprinkle topping evenly over sweet potatoes.*

5. Bake 25 to 30 minutes or until sweet potatoes are heated through. For crisper topping, broil 5 inches from heat 2 to 3 minutes or until golden brown.   ***Makes 6 to 8 servings***

*At this point, Sweet Potato Gratin may be covered and refrigerated up to 1 day. Let stand at room temperature 1 hour before baking.

Sweet Potato Gratin

Candied Pineapple Yams

5 pounds yams or sweet potatoes, washed and pierced with fork
½ cup DOLE® Pineapple Juice
¼ cup margarine, melted
½ teaspoon salt
½ teaspoon pumpkin pie spice
½ cup packed brown sugar
1 container (16 ounces) DOLE® Fresh Pineapple, cut into slices

• Place yams on foil-lined baking sheet. Bake at 350°F, 90 minutes or until yams are tender when pricked with fork.

• Spoon out baked yams from skins and place into large mixing bowl. Add pineapple juice, margarine, salt and pumpkin pie spice. Beat until fluffy.

• Spoon mixture into lightly greased 13×9-inch baking dish. Sprinkle with brown sugar. Arrange pineapple slices over yams. Continue baking at 350°F, 15 minutes or until hot.   *Makes 10 servings*

PREP TIME: 90 minutes

Corn Maque Choux

2 tablespoons butter or margarine
½ cup chopped onion
½ cup chopped green pepper
4 cups whole kernel corn (canned, fresh or frozen, thawed)
1 medium tomato, chopped
¼ teaspoon salt
½ teaspoon TABASCO® brand Pepper Sauce

Melt butter over medium heat in 3-quart saucepan. Add onion and green pepper; cook 5 minutes or until tender, stirring frequently. Stir in corn, tomato, salt and TABASCO® Sauce. Reduce heat and simmer 10 to 15 minutes or until corn is tender.   *Makes 3 cups*

Creamy Succotash

1 (15-ounce) can lima beans
1 (11-ounce) can whole kernel corn with red and green bell peppers
1 tablespoon butter or margarine
1 tablespoon flour
1½ teaspoons HERB-OX® instant chicken bouillon granules
⅛ teaspoon salt
¼ teaspoon pepper
¾ cup half-and-half
2 green onions, sliced

In medium saucepan, heat lima beans and corn until warmed through; drain. Stir in butter until melted. Add flour, bouillon, salt and pepper. Stir in half-and-half. Cook until thickened and bubbly. Stir in green onions.

Makes 6 servings

PREP TIME: 10 minutes
TOTAL TIME: 20 minutes

Cornbread Stuffing with Sausage and Apple

⅓ cup pecan pieces
1 pound bulk pork sausage
1 large Jonathan apple
1⅓ cups chicken broth
¼ cup apple juice
6 ounces seasoned cornbread stuffing mix

1. Preheat oven to 300°F. Place pecan pieces in shallow baking pan. Bake 6 to 8 minutes or until lightly browned, stirring frequently.

2. Place sausage in large skillet; cook over high heat 10 minutes or until meat is no longer pink, stirring to break up meat. Pour off drippings.

3. Meanwhile, coarsely chop apple. Place in 3-quart saucepan. Add broth, apple juice and seasoning packet from stuffing mix. Bring to a boil, uncovered, over high heat. Remove from heat and stir in stuffing mix. Cover; let stand 3 to 5 minutes or until stuffing is moist and tender.

4. Stir sausage into stuffing. Spoon into serving bowl and top with nuts.

Makes 4 servings

PREP AND COOK TIME: 20 minutes

Cornbread Stuffing with Sausage and Apple

HEIRLOOM
Cakes & Pies

Carnation® Key Lime Pie

1 *prepared* 9-inch (6 ounces) graham cracker crumb crust
1 can (14 ounces) NESTLÉ® CARNATION® Sweetened Condensed Milk
½ cup (about 3 medium limes) fresh lime juice
1 teaspoon grated lime peel
2 cups frozen whipped topping, thawed
    Lime peel twists or lime slices (optional)

BEAT sweetened condensed milk and lime juice in small mixer bowl until combined; stir in lime peel. Pour into crust; spread with whipped topping. Refrigerate for 2 hours or until set. Garnish with lime peel twists.

Makes 8 servings

Carnation® Key Lime Pie

Chess Pie

CRUST

1 unbaked Classic CRISCO® Single Crust (page 155)

FILLING

3 cups sugar
½ cup butter or margarine, softened
5 eggs, lightly beaten
3 tablespoons cornmeal
2 teaspoons vanilla
⅛ teaspoon salt
1 cup milk

1. For crust, prepare as directed. Do not bake. Heat oven to 325°F.

2. For filling, combine sugar and butter in large bowl. Beat at low speed of electric mixer until blended. Beat in eggs, cornmeal, vanilla and salt. Add milk. Beat at low speed until blended. Pour into unbaked pie crust.

3. Bake at 325°F for 1 hour to 1 hour 20 minutes or until filling is set. Cover edge of pie with foil, if necessary, to prevent overbrowning. *Do not overbake.* Cool to room temperature before serving. Refrigerate leftover pie.

Makes 1 pie

Classic Crisco® Single Crust

1⅓ cups all-purpose flour
½ teaspoon salt
½ CRISCO® Stick or ½ cup CRISCO® all-vegetable shortening
3 tablespoons cold water

1. Spoon flour into measuring cup and level. Combine flour and salt in medium bowl.

2. Cut in ½ cup shortening using pastry blender or 2 knives until all flour is blended to form pea-size chunks.

3. Sprinkle with water, 1 tablespoon at a time. Toss lightly with fork until dough forms a ball.

4. Press dough between hands to form 5- to 6-inch "pancake." Flour rolling surface and rolling pin lightly. Roll dough into circle. Trim circle 1 inch larger than upside-down pie plate. Carefully remove trimmed dough. Set aside to reroll and use for pastry cutout garnish, if desired.

5. Fold dough into quarters. Unfold and press into pie plate. Fold edge under. Flute.

6. **For recipes using a baked pie crust,** heat oven to 425°F. Prick bottom and side thoroughly with fork (50 times) to prevent shrinkage. Bake at 425°F for 10 to 15 minutes or until lightly browned.

7. **For recipes using an unbaked pie crust,** follow directions given for that recipe.   *Makes 1 (9-inch) single crust*

Classic Pecan Pie

3 eggs
1 cup sugar
1 cup KARO® Light or Dark Corn Syrup
2 tablespoons margarine or butter, melted
1 teaspoon vanilla
1¼ cups pecans
Easy-As-Pie Crust (page 158) *or* 1 (9-inch) frozen deep-dish pie crust*

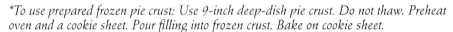

To use prepared frozen pie crust: Use 9-inch deep-dish pie crust. Do not thaw. Preheat oven and a cookie sheet. Pour filling into frozen crust. Bake on cookie sheet.

1. Preheat oven to 350°F.

2. In medium bowl with fork beat eggs slightly. Add sugar, Karo Corn Syrup, margarine and vanilla; stir until well blended. Stir in pecans. Pour into pie crust.

3. Bake 50 to 55 minutes or until knife inserted halfway between center and edge comes out clean. Cool on wire rack.   *Makes 8 servings*

ALMOND AMARETTO PIE: Substitute 1 cup sliced almonds for pecans. Add 2 tablespoons almond flavored liqueur and ½ teaspoon almond extract to filling.

BUTTERSCOTCH PECAN PIE: Omit margarine; add ¼ cup heavy or whipping cream to filling.

CHOCOLATE CHIP WALNUT PIE: Substitute 1 cup walnuts, coarsely chopped, for pecans. Sprinkle ½ cup semisweet chocolate chips over bottom of pie crust. Carefully pour filling into pie crust.

PREP TIME: 10 minutes
BAKE TIME: 55 minutes

Classic Pecan Pie

Easy-As-Pie Crust

1¼ **cups flour**
⅛ **teaspoon salt**
½ **cup margarine or butter**
2 **tablespoons cold water**

1. In medium bowl mix flour and salt. With pastry blender or 2 knives, cut in margarine until mixture resembles fine crumbs.

2. Sprinkle water over flour mixture while tossing with fork to blend well. Press dough firmly into ball.

3. On lightly floured surface roll out to 12-inch circle. Fit loosely into 9-inch pie plate. Trim and flute edge. Fill and bake as recipe directs.

Makes 1 (9-inch) pie crust

BAKED PIE SHELL: Preheat oven to 450°F. Pierce pie crust thoroughly with fork. Bake 10 to 15 minutes or until light brown.

PREP TIME: 15 minutes

*The butter must be chilled before making
pastry dough in order for it to be evenly distributed
throughout the flour. Also, ice water helps to keep the
butter solid. Avoid overworking the dough or the pastry
will be tough. Wrap the ball of dough in plastic wrap
and refrigerate it for at least one hour. Chilling the
dough makes it easier to handle and helps prevent
shrinkage during baking.*

Mississippi Mud Pie

1 *prepared* 9-inch (6 ounces) chocolate crumb crust
1 cup powdered sugar
1 cup (6 ounces) NESTLÉ® TOLL HOUSE® Semi-Sweet
   Chocolate Morsels
¼ cup (½ stick) butter or margarine, cut up
¼ cup heavy whipping cream
2 tablespoons light corn syrup
1 teaspoon vanilla extract
¾ cup chopped nuts, *divided* (optional)
2 pints coffee ice cream, softened slightly, *divided*
   Whipped cream (optional)

HEAT sugar, morsels, butter, cream and corn syrup in small, *heavy-duty* saucepan over low heat, stirring constantly, until butter is melted and mixture is smooth. Remove from heat. Stir in vanilla extract. Cool until slightly warm.

DRIZZLE *⅓ cup* chocolate sauce in bottom of crust; sprinkle with *¼ cup* nuts. Layer *1 pint* ice cream, scooping thin slices with a large spoon; freeze for 1 hour. Repeat with *⅓ cup* sauce, *¼ cup* nuts and *remaining* ice cream. Drizzle with *remaining* sauce; top with *remaining* nuts. Freeze for 2 hours or until firm. Top with whipped cream before serving.   *Makes 8 servings*

Southern Secret

If you don't have a chocolate pie crust
to make this delicious pie, use ingredients from
your kitchen to quickly make a crust. Combine
1½ cups graham cracker crumbs, 2 tablespoons sugar
and 2 tablespoons unsweetened cocoa powder in a
9-inch pie pan. Stir in ¼ cup melted butter. Press
mixture evenly onto the bottom of the pan.
Bake 8 minutes. Cool completely.

Farmhouse Lemon Meringue Pie

1 frozen pie crust, baked according to package directions
4 eggs, at room temperature
3 tablespoons lemon juice
2 tablespoons butter
2 teaspoons grated lemon peel
3 drops yellow food coloring (optional)
⅔ cup sugar, divided
1 cup cold water
¼ cup cornstarch
⅛ teaspoon salt
¼ teaspoon vanilla

1. Preheat oven to 425°F.

2. Separate eggs, discarding 2 egg yolks; set aside. Mix lemon juice, butter, lemon peel and food coloring, if desired, in small bowl; set aside.

3. Reserve 2 tablespoons sugar. Combine water, remaining sugar, cornstarch and salt in medium saucepan; whisk until smooth. Heat over medium-high heat, whisking constantly, until mixture begins to boil. Reduce heat to medium. Continue to boil 1 minute, stirring constantly; remove from heat.

4. Stir ¼ cup boiling sugar mixture into egg yolks; whisk constantly until completely blended. Slowly whisk egg yolk mixture back into sugar mixture. Cook over medium heat 3 minutes, whisking constantly. Remove from heat; stir in lemon juice mixture until well blended. Pour into baked pie crust.

5. Beat egg whites in large bowl with electric mixer at high speed until soft peaks form. Gradually beat in reserved 2 tablespoons sugar and vanilla; beat until stiff peaks form. Spread meringue over pie filling with rubber spatula, making sure meringue completely covers filling and touches edge of pie crust.

6. Bake 15 minutes. Remove from oven; cool completely on wire rack. Cover with plastic wrap; refrigerate 8 hours or overnight until pie is set and thoroughly chilled. Garnish, if desired.   *Makes 8 servings*

Farmhouse Lemon Meringue Pie

The "Ultimate" Peanut Butter Whoopie Pies

PIES

½ Butter Flavor CRISCO® Stick or ½ cup Butter Flavor CRISCO®
   all-vegetable shortening plus additional for greasing

1 cup milk

1 tablespoon white vinegar

1 cup granulated sugar

1 cup firmly packed brown sugar

¾ cup JIF® Crunchy Peanut Butter

1 cup boiling water

1 teaspoon vanilla

4 cups all-purpose flour

½ cup unsweetened cocoa powder

2 teaspoons baking soda

½ teaspoon baking powder

½ teaspoon salt

FILLING

½ cup milk

3 tablespoons all-purpose flour

2 cups confectioners' sugar

½ Butter Flavor CRISCO® Stick or ½ cup Butter Flavor CRISCO®
   all-vegetable shortening

½ cup JIF® Creamy Peanut Butter

1 teaspoon vanilla

1. Heat oven to 425°F. Grease baking sheet with shortening. Place sheets of foil on countertop for cooling pies.

2. For pies, combine 1 cup milk and vinegar in small microwavable bowl. Microwave at HIGH to warm slightly (or on rangetop in small saucepan on medium heat). Mixture will appear separated and curdled.

3. Combine granulated sugar, brown sugar and crunchy peanut butter in large bowl. Beat at medium speed with electric mixer until crumbly.

4. Combine remaining ½ cup shortening and boiling water. Stir to melt shortening. Add to peanut butter mixture along with milk mixture and vanilla. Beat at low speed. Mixture will be very fluid and somewhat separated.

5. Combine 4 cups flour, cocoa, baking soda, baking powder and salt. Stir well. Add all at once to peanut butter mixture. Beat at low speed until mixture is blended and resembles thick cake batter. Let stand 20 minutes. Drop by rounded measuring tablespoonfuls 2 inches apart onto prepared baking sheet.

6. Bake in upper half of oven for 8 to 10 minutes or until set. *Do not overbake.* Cool 2 minutes on baking sheet. Remove pies to foil to cool completely.

7. For filling, combine ½ cup milk and 3 tablespoons flour in small saucepan. Cook and stir on medium heat until thickened. Cool completely. Add confectioners' sugar, ½ cup shortening, creamy peanut butter and vanilla. Beat at low speed until blended. Beat at high until smooth. Refrigerate until ready to use. Spread filling on bottoms of half of the pies. Top with remaining halves. Press together gently.   *Makes 2½ dozen whoopie pies*

Southern Secret

Whoopie pies are little chocolate cakes with creamy filling. They are great for birthday celebrations, and kids love to help make these treats—especially spreading the cream filling between the chocolate cakes. Serving a big glass of milk is almost mandatory with these soft cookie sandwiches.

Georgia Peach Pie

CRUST
1 unbaked 10-inch Classic CRISCO® Double Crust (page 166)

FILLING
1 can (29 ounces) yellow cling peaches in heavy syrup
3 tablespoons reserved peach syrup
3 tablespoons cornstarch
1 cup sugar, divided
3 eggs
⅓ cup buttermilk
½ cup butter or margarine, melted
1 teaspoon vanilla

GLAZE
2 tablespoons butter or margarine, melted
Additional sugar

1. Prepare Crust. Heat oven to 400°F.

2. For Filling, drain peaches, reserving 3 tablespoons syrup; set aside. Cut peaches into small pieces; place in large bowl. Combine cornstarch and 3 tablespoons sugar in medium bowl. Add 3 tablespoons reserved peach syrup; mix well. Add remaining sugar, eggs and buttermilk; mix well. Stir in ½ cup melted butter and vanilla. Pour over peaches; stir until peaches are coated. Pour filling into unbaked pie crust. Moisten pastry edge with water.

3. Cover pie with top crust. Fold top edge under bottom crust; flute with fingers or fork. Cut slits or designs in top crust to allow steam to escape.

4. For Glaze, brush top crust with 2 tablespoons melted butter. Sprinkle with additional sugar.

5. Bake at 400°F for 45 minutes or until filling in center is bubbly and crust is golden brown. *Do not overbake.* Cool to room temperature before serving.

Makes 1 (10-inch) pie

Georgia Peach Pie

10-inch Classic Crisco® Double Crust

2⅔ cups all-purpose flour
1 teaspoon salt
¾ CRISCO® Stick or ¾ cup CRISCO® all-vegetable shortening
7 to 8 tablespoons cold water (or more as needed)

1. Spoon flour into measuring cup and level. Combine flour and salt in medium bowl.

2. Cut in ¾ cup shortening using pastry blender or 2 knives until all flour is blended to form pea-size chunks.

3. Sprinkle with water, 1 tablespoon at a time. Toss lightly with fork until dough forms a ball. Divide dough in half.

4. Press dough between hands to form two 5- to 6-inch "pancakes." Flour rolling surface and rolling pin lightly. Roll both halves of dough into circle. Trim one circle of dough 1 inch larger than upside-down pie plate. Carefully remove trimmed dough. Set aside to reroll and use for pastry cutout garnish, if desired.

5. Fold dough into quarters. Unfold and press into pie plate. Trim edge even with plate. Add desired filling to unbaked crust. Moisten pastry edge with water. Lift top crust onto filled pie. Trim ½ inch beyond edge of pie plate. Fold top edge under bottom crust. Flute. Cut slits in top crust to allow steam to escape. Follow baking directions given for that recipe.

Makes 1 double crust

Apple Brandy Praline Pie

Praline Topping (recipe follows)
¼ **cup sugar**
3 **tablespoons all-purpose flour**
¼ **teaspoon salt**
3 **eggs**
½ **cup KARO® Light or Dark Corn Syrup**
¼ **cup (½ stick) margarine or butter, melted**
2 **tablespoons apple or plain brandy**
2 **medium apples, peeled and thinly sliced**
1 **unbaked (9-inch) pie crust**

1. Prepare Praline Topping; set aside.

2. In large bowl combine sugar, flour and salt. Beat in eggs, corn syrup, margarine and brandy. Stir in apples. Pour into pie crust.

3. Sprinkle with topping.

4. Bake in 350°F oven 45 to 50 minutes or until puffed and set. Cool on wire rack.   *Makes 8 servings*

PRALINE TOPPING: In small bowl combine 1 cup coarsely chopped pecans, ¼ cup all-purpose flour, ¼ cup brown sugar and 2 tablespoons softened margarine or butter. Mix with fork until crumbly.

PREP TIME: 30 minutes
BAKE TIME: 50 minutes, plus cooling

Sweet Potato Pecan Pie

1 pound sweet potatoes or yams, cooked and peeled
¼ cup (½ stick) butter or margarine, softened
1 (14-ounce) can EAGLE BRAND® Sweetened Condensed Milk
   (NOT evaporated milk)
1 egg
1 teaspoon grated orange peel
1 teaspoon ground cinnamon
1 teaspoon vanilla extract
½ teaspoon ground nutmeg
¼ teaspoon salt
1 (6-ounce) graham cracker crumb pie crust
   Pecan Topping (recipe follows)

1. Preheat oven to 425°F. In large mixing bowl, beat hot sweet potatoes and butter until smooth. Add EAGLE BRAND® and remaining ingredients except crust and Pecan Topping; mix well. Pour into crust.

2. Bake 20 minutes. Meanwhile, prepare Pecan Topping.

3. Remove pie from oven; reduce oven temperature to 350°F. Spoon Pecan Topping over pie.

4. Bake 25 minutes longer or until set. Cool. Serve warm or at room temperature. Garnish with orange zest twist, if desired. Refrigerate leftovers.

Makes 1 pie

PECAN TOPPING: In small mixing bowl, beat 1 egg, 2 tablespoons firmly packed light brown sugar, 2 tablespoons dark corn syrup, 1 tablespoon melted butter and ½ teaspoon maple flavoring. Stir in 1 cup chopped pecans.

PREP TIME: 30 minutes
BAKE TIME: 45 minutes

 *168*

Sweet Potato Pecan Pie

Brown-Eyed Susan Sweet Potato Cake

CAKE

2¼ cups all-purpose flour
1 tablespoon baking powder
1 teaspoon baking soda
1 teaspoon salt
1 teaspoon ground cinnamon
½ teaspoon ground ginger
1 can (15 ounces) mashed sweet potatoes or 1 can (15 ounces) unsweetened sweet potatoes, rinsed, drained and mashed
1 cup granulated sugar
½ cup packed dark brown sugar
3 large eggs
1 cup vegetable oil
1 cup (6 ounces) NESTLÉ® TOLL HOUSE® Semi-Sweet Chocolate Morsels
½ cup chopped pecans
½ cup water

CREAMY PREMIER WHITE ICING

¾ cup NESTLÉ® TOLL HOUSE® Premier White Morsels
1½ tablespoons butter or margarine
½ cup (4 ounces) cream cheese, softened
⅓ cup sour cream
¾ teaspoon vanilla extract
¼ teaspoon almond extract (optional)
3 to 4 cups powdered sugar

FOR CAKE

PREHEAT oven to 350°F. Lightly grease and flour two 9-inch-round cake pans or one 13×9-inch baking pan.

continued on page 172

Brown-Eyed Susan Sweet Potato Cake

Brown-Eyed Susan Sweet Potato Cake, continued

COMBINE flour, baking powder, baking soda, salt, cinnamon and ginger in small bowl. Combine sweet potatoes, granulated sugar and brown sugar in large bowl. Add eggs, one at a time, beating well after each addition. Add oil; beat until well blended. Stir in morsels, pecans and water. Stir in flour mixture; mix until blended. Pour into prepared pan(s).

BAKE for 35 to 40 minutes or until wooden pick inserted in center comes out clean. Cool completely in pan(s) on wire rack(s). For layer cakes, remove from pans after 10 minutes. Frost with Creamy Premier White Icing.

FOR CREAMY PREMIER WHITE ICING

MICROWAVE morsels and butter in small, uncovered, microwave-safe bowl on MEDIUM-HIGH (70%) power for 1 minute. STIR. Morsels may retain some of their original shape. If necessary, microwave at additional 10- to 15-second intervals, stirring just until morsels are melted. Cool to room temperature.

BEAT cream cheese and sour cream into morsel mixture until creamy. Add vanilla extract and almond extract. Gradually beat in powdered sugar until mixture reaches spreading consistency. Makes about 3 cups icing.

Makes 12 servings

Southern Jam Cake

CAKE

¾ cup butter or margarine, softened
1 cup granulated sugar
3 eggs
1 cup (12-ounce jar) SMUCKER'S® Seedless Blackberry Jam
2½ cups all-purpose flour
1 teaspoon baking soda
1 teaspoon ground cinnamon
1 teaspoon ground cloves
1 teaspoon ground allspice
1 teaspoon ground nutmeg
¾ cup buttermilk

CARAMEL ICING (OPTIONAL)

2 tablespoons butter
½ cup firmly packed brown sugar
3 tablespoons milk
1¾ cups powdered sugar

Grease and flour tube pan. Combine ¾ cup butter and granulated sugar; beat until light and fluffy. Add eggs one at a time, beating well after each addition. Fold in jam.

Combine flour, baking soda, cinnamon, cloves, allspice and nutmeg; mix well. Add to batter alternately with buttermilk, stirring just enough to blend after each addition. Spoon mixture into prepared pan.

Bake at 350°F for 50 minutes or until toothpick inserted in center comes out clean. Cool in pan for 10 minutes. Remove from pan; cool completely.

In saucepan, melt 2 tablespoons butter; stir in brown sugar. Cook, stirring constantly, until mixture boils; remove from heat. Cool 5 minutes. Stir in milk; blend in powdered sugar. Frost cake. ***Makes 12 to 16 servings***

Sour Cream Pound Cake

1 orange
1 cup (2 sticks) butter, softened
2¾ cups sugar
1 tablespoon vanilla
6 eggs
3 cups all-purpose flour
½ teaspoon salt
¼ teaspoon baking soda
1 cup sour cream
Citrus Topping (page 176)

1. Preheat oven to 325°F. Grease 10-inch tube pan. Finely grate peel of orange (not white pith) to measure 2 teaspoons; set aside.

2. Beat butter in large bowl with electric mixer at medium speed until creamy, scraping down side of bowl once. Gradually add sugar, beating until light and fluffy. Beat in vanilla and orange peel. Add eggs, 1 at a time, beating 1 minute after each addition.

3. Combine flour, salt and baking soda in small bowl. Add to butter mixture alternately with sour cream, beginning and ending with flour mixture. Beat well after each addition. Pour into prepared pan.

4. Bake 1 hour 15 minutes or until toothpick inserted near center comes out clean.

5. Meanwhile, prepare Citrus Topping. Spoon over hot cake; cool in pan 15 minutes. Remove from pan to wire rack; cool completely.

Makes 10 to 12 servings

Sour Cream Pound Cake

Citrus Topping

2 oranges
2 teaspoons salt
Water
½ cup sugar, divided
⅓ cup lemon juice
1 teaspoon vanilla

1. Grate peel of oranges (not white pith) to measure 2 tablespoons. Cut oranges in half. Squeeze juice from oranges to measure ⅓ cup.

2. Combine orange peel and salt in medium saucepan. Add enough water to cover. Bring to a boil over high heat. Boil 2 minutes. Drain in fine-meshed sieve. Return orange peel to saucepan.

3. Add orange juice and ¼ cup sugar to saucepan. Bring to a boil over high heat. Reduce heat; simmer 10 minutes. Remove from heat. Add remaining ¼ cup sugar, lemon juice and vanilla; stir until smooth.

Makes about ½ cup topping

Kentucky Bourbon Cake

      4 cups all-purpose flour
      2 teaspoons ground nutmeg
  1½ teaspoons baking powder
      3 cups chopped pecans
      2 cups mixed candied fruit (about 1 pound)
      2 cups raisins
      2 cups orange marmalade
      2 cups sugar
  1½ cups (3 sticks) butter, softened
      6 eggs
  ½ cup molasses
  ¾ cup bourbon

1. Preheat oven to 300°F. Grease two 10-inch tube pans. Line bottoms of pans with waxed paper; set aside.

2. Sift flour, nutmeg and baking powder into medium bowl; set aside. Combine pecans, candied fruit, raisins and marmalade in large bowl; add 1 cup flour mixture. Stir to coat well.

3. Beat sugar and butter 2 minutes in large bowl with electric mixer at medium speed until fluffy. Beat in eggs, one at a time. Stir in molasses. Add half remaining flour mixture, then bourbon, beating well after each addition. Beat in remaining flour mixture until well blended. Stir in fruit mixture. Pour into prepared pans.

4. Bake 2 hours or until toothpick inserted near centers comes out clean. Cool 10 minutes. Remove from pans to wire racks; cool completely. Wrap cakes in cheesecloth soaked with bourbon. Wrap in foil and let mellow for at least 2 days.   *Makes 24 servings*

TIP: Sprinkle an extra ¼ cup bourbon over cakes after 1 day for more flavor.

SWEET

Temptations

Ambrosia

1 can (20 ounces) DOLE® Pineapple Chunks
1 can (11 or 15 ounces) DOLE® Mandarin Oranges
1 firm, large DOLE® Banana, sliced (optional)
1½ cups DOLE® Seedless Grapes
1 cup miniature marshmallows
1 cup flaked coconut
½ cup pecan halves or coarsely chopped nuts
1 cup vanilla yogurt or sour cream
1 tablespoon brown sugar

• Drain pineapple chunks and mandarin oranges. In large bowl, combine pineapple chunks, mandarin oranges, banana, grapes, marshmallows, coconut and nuts. In 1-quart measure, combine yogurt and brown sugar. Stir into fruit mixture. Refrigerate, covered, 1 hour or overnight.

Makes 4 servings

Ambrosia

Crunch Peach Cobbler

⅓ cup plus 1 tablespoon granulated sugar, divided
1 tablespoon cornstarch
1 can (29 ounces) *or* 2 cans (16 ounces each) cling peach slices
    in syrup, drained, reserving ¾ cup syrup
½ teaspoon vanilla
2 cups all-purpose flour, divided
½ cup packed light brown sugar
⅓ cup uncooked old-fashioned or quick oats
¼ cup (½ stick) butter, melted
½ teaspoon ground cinnamon
½ teaspoon salt
½ cup shortening
4 to 5 tablespoons cold water
    Whipped cream for garnish

1. Combine ⅓ cup granulated sugar and cornstarch in small saucepan.
Slowly add reserved peach syrup. Stir well. Add vanilla. Cook over low heat,
stirring constantly, until thickened. Set aside.

2. For crumb topping, combine ½ cup flour, brown sugar, oats, butter and
cinnamon in small bowl; stir until mixture forms coarse crumbs. Set aside.

3. Preheat oven to 350°F. Combine remaining 1½ cups flour, remaining
1 tablespoon granulated sugar and salt in small bowl. Cut in shortening with
pastry blender or 2 knives until mixture forms pea-sized pieces. Sprinkle
water, 1 tablespoon at a time, over flour mixture. Toss lightly with fork until
mixture holds together. Press together to form a ball.

4. Roll out dough into 10-inch square, ⅛ inch thick. Fold dough in half, then
in half again. Carefully place folded dough in center of 8-inch square baking
dish. Unfold and press onto bottom and about 1 inch up sides of dish.
Arrange peaches over crust. Pour sauce over peaches. Sprinkle with crumb
topping.

5. Bake 45 minutes. Serve warm or at room temperature with whipped
cream. ***Makes about 6 servings***

Crunch Peach Cobbler

Strawberry Shortcakes

SHORTCAKES

2¼ cups all-purpose flour
2 tablespoons granulated sugar
1 tablespoon baking powder
½ teaspoon salt
½ CRISCO® Stick or ½ cup CRISCO® all-vegetable shortening
1 large egg, beaten
¾ cup milk

FILLING

1 quart strawberries, hulled and sliced
Granulated sugar to taste
1 cup whipping cream, whipped stiff

1. Heat oven to 425°F. Combine flour, sugar, baking powder and salt in medium bowl. Cut in ½ cup shortening using pastry blender (or two knives) until flour is blended to form pea-size chunks. Make well in center. Combine egg and milk. Pour into well. Stir with fork 25 to 30 strokes.

2. Turn dough onto lightly floured surface. Roll dough ½ inch thick. Cut with floured 4-inch cutter. Place 2 inches apart on ungreased baking sheet.

3. Bake at 425°F for 11 to 13 minutes, or until lightly browned. *Do not overbake.* Cool. Cut shortcakes in half with bread knife.

4. For filling, combine strawberries and sugar. Spoon over bottom halves of shortcakes. Top with whipped cream and shortcake tops.

Makes 6 servings

NOTE: The shortcakes are best if made within a few hours of serving.

PREP TIME: 25 minutes
TOTAL TIME: 35 minutes

Bread Pudding
with Southern Whiskey Sauce

½ (1-pound) loaf day-old* French or Italian bread
⅔ cup granulated sugar
⅓ cup packed brown sugar
¾ teaspoon ground cinnamon
¼ teaspoon ground nutmeg
6 eggs
3 cups milk
1 tablespoon vanilla
¾ cup raisins
Southern Whiskey Sauce (recipe follows)

For best results, bread should be slightly stale. Cut fresh bread into ½-inch-thick slices; place on tray or baking sheet. Let stand at room temperature 30 to 60 minutes or until slightly dry.

1. Preheat oven to 350°F. Grease 12×8-inch baking dish. Cut bread into ½-inch slices; cut slices into ½-inch cubes to measure 8 cups. Place cubes into prepared baking dish.

2. Combine sugars, cinnamon and nutmeg in large bowl. Beat eggs in medium bowl until frothy; stir in milk and vanilla until blended. Add egg mixture to sugar mixture; stir until well blended. Sprinkle raisins over bread cubes. Pour egg mixture over bread cubes. Push bread into liquid to moisten each piece. Let stand 5 minutes.

3. Bake 45 to 50 minutes or until set and knife inserted in center comes out clean. Prepare whiskey sauce. Serve warm sauce over warm bread pudding.

Makes 8 servings

SOUTHERN WHISKEY SAUCE: Combine ¾ cup sugar and 2 teaspoons cornstarch in medium saucepan. Stir in ¾ cup half-and-half or whipping cream; cook and stir over medium-low heat until thick and bubbly. Cook 1 minute more; remove from heat. Carefully stir in 2 tablespoons bourbon whiskey, ⅛ teaspoon ground cinnamon and dash of salt. Cool slightly. Store covered in refrigerator up to two days.

Mixed Berry Cobbler

1 package (16 ounces) frozen mixed berries
¾ cup granulated sugar
2 tablespoons quick-cooking tapioca
2 teaspoons grated fresh lemon peel
1½ cups all-purpose flour
½ cup packed brown sugar
2¼ teaspoons baking powder
¼ teaspoon ground nutmeg
¾ cup milk
⅓ cup butter, melted
Ice cream (optional)

SLOW COOKER DIRECTIONS

1. Stir together berries, granulated sugar, tapioca and lemon peel in slow cooker.

2. Combine flour, brown sugar, baking powder and nutmeg in medium bowl. Add milk and butter; stir just until blended. Drop spoonfuls on top of berry mixture.

3. Cover; cook on LOW 4 hours. Uncover; let stand about 30 minutes. Serve with ice cream, if desired. **Makes 8 servings**

PREP TIME: 10 minutes
COOK TIME: 4 hours
STAND TIME: 30 minutes

Mixed Berry Cobbler

Bananas Foster

6 tablespoons I CAN'T BELIEVE IT'S NOT BUTTER!® Spread
3 tablespoons firmly packed brown sugar
4 medium ripe bananas, sliced diagonally
2 tablespoons dark rum or brandy (optional)
   Vanilla ice cream

In 12-inch skillet, bring I Can't Believe It's Not Butter!® Spread, brown sugar and bananas to a boil. Cook 2 minutes, stirring gently. Carefully add rum to center of pan and cook 15 seconds. Serve hot banana mixture over scoops of ice cream and top, if desired, with sweetened whipped cream.

Makes 4 servings

NOTE: Recipe can be halved.

PREP TIME: 5 minutes
COOK TIME: 5 minutes

*For a last minute dessert, try Bananas Foster.
Impress your family and friends with this elegant, quick
dessert made with with ingredients you probably
already have in the kitchen. Top with a sprinkle of
cinnamon or chopped nuts. Yum!*

Bananas Foster

Banana Pudding

60 to 70 vanilla wafers*
1 cup granulated sugar
3 tablespoons cornstarch
¼ teaspoon salt
2 cans (12 fluid ounces *each*) NESTLÉ® CARNATION® Evaporated Milk
2 eggs, lightly beaten
3 tablespoons butter, cut into pieces
1½ teaspoons vanilla extract
5 ripe but firm large bananas, cut into ¼-inch slices
1 container (8 ounces) frozen whipped topping, thawed

A 12-ounce box of vanilla wafers contains about 88 wafers.

LINE bottom and side of 2½-quart glass bowl with about 40 wafers.

COMBINE sugar, cornstarch and salt in medium saucepan. Gradually stir in evaporated milk to dissolve cornstarch. Whisk in eggs. Add butter. Cook over medium heat, stirring constantly, until the mixture begins to thicken. Reduce heat to low; bring to a simmer and cook for 1 minute, stirring constantly. Remove from heat. Stir in vanilla extract. Let cool slightly.

POUR *half* of pudding over wafers. Top with *half* of bananas. Layer *remaining* vanilla wafers over bananas. Combine *remaining* pudding and bananas; spoon over wafers. Refrigerate for at least 4 hours. Top with whipped topping. ***Makes 8 servings***

Dreamy Divinity

3½ cups DOMINO® Granulated Sugar
⅔ cup water
⅔ cup light corn syrup
⅓ teaspoon salt
3 egg whites, beaten until stiff
1½ teaspoons vanilla extract
    Food coloring, candied cherries and chopped nuts (optional)

Combine sugar, water, corn syrup and salt in saucepan. Heat, stirring occasionally, until sugar dissolves. Wipe down sugar crystals from side of pan as necessary with pastry brush dipped in water. Boil syrup mixture, without stirring, until mixture reaches 265°F or hard-ball stage on candy thermometer.

Gradually beat hot syrup into beaten egg whites. Add vanilla. Tint with food coloring, if desired. Continue beating until candy holds shape. Drop by teaspoonfuls onto buttered baking sheet or plate. Garnish with cherries and nuts as desired. When firm, store in airtight container.

Makes 50 pieces (1½ pounds)

Reese's® Peanut Butter and Milk Chocolate Chip Tassies

¾ cup (1½ sticks) butter, softened
1 package (3 ounces) cream cheese, softened
1½ cups all-purpose flour
¾ cup sugar, divided
1 egg, slightly beaten
2 tablespoons butter or margarine, melted
¼ teaspoon lemon juice
¼ teaspoon vanilla extract
1¾ cups (11-ounce package) REESE'S® Peanut Butter and Milk
  Chocolate Chips, divided
2 teaspoons shortening (do not use butter, margarine, spread or oil)

1. Beat ¾ cup butter and cream cheese in medium bowl; add flour and ¼ cup sugar, beating until well blended. Cover; refrigerate about 1 hour or until dough is firm. Shape dough into 1-inch balls; press each ball onto bottom and up sides of about 36 small muffin cups (1¾ inches in diameter).

2. Heat oven to 350°F. Combine egg, remaining ½ cup sugar, melted butter, lemon juice and vanilla in small bowl; stir until smooth. Set aside ⅓ cup chips; add remainder to egg mixture. Evenly fill muffin cups with chip mixture.

3. Bake 20 to 25 minutes or until filling is set and lightly browned. Cool completely; remove from pan to wire rack.

4. Combine reserved ⅓ cup chips and shortening in small microwave-safe bowl. Microwave at HIGH (100% power) 30 seconds; stir. If necessary, microwave additional 15 seconds at a time, stirring after each heating, until chips are melted and mixture is smooth when stirred. Drizzle over tops of tassies.   ***Makes 3 dozen cookies***

Reese's® Peanut Butter and Milk Chocolate Chip Tassies

Kentucky Oatmeal-Jam Cookies

½ Butter Flavor CRISCO® Stick or ½ cup Butter Flavor CRISCO®
all-vegetable shortening plus additional for greasing

¾ cup sugar

1 egg

½ cup SMUCKER'S® Strawberry Jam

¼ cup buttermilk*

1 teaspoon vanilla

1 cup all-purpose flour

½ cup unsweetened cocoa powder

1 teaspoon ground cinnamon

½ teaspoon baking soda

¼ teaspoon nutmeg

¼ teaspoon ground cloves

1½ cups quick oats (not instant or old-fashioned), uncooked

½ cup raisins

½ cup chopped pecans (optional)

About 24 pecan halves (optional)

*You can substitute ¾ teaspoon lemon juice or vinegar plus enough milk to make ¼ cup
for buttermilk. Stir. Wait 5 minutes before using.*

1. Heat oven to 350°F. Grease baking sheet. Place foil on countertop for
cooling cookies.

2. Combine ½ cup shortening, sugar, egg, jam, buttermilk and vanilla in
large bowl. Beat at medium speed of electric mixer until well blended.

3. Combine flour, cocoa, cinnamon, baking soda, nutmeg and cloves. Mix
into creamed mixture at low speed until blended. Stir in oats, raisins and
chopped nuts with spoon.

4. Drop 2 tablespoonfuls of dough in a mound on baking sheet. Repeat for
each cookie, spacing 3 inches apart. Top each with pecan half.

5. Bake 10 to 12 minutes or until set. *Do not overbake.* Cool 2 minutes on
baking sheet. Remove cookies to foil to cool completely.

Makes about 2 dozen cookies

Kentucky Oatmeal-Jam Cookies

Peanut Gems

2½ **cups all-purpose flour**
  1 **teaspoon baking powder**
  ⅛ **teaspoon salt**
  1 **cup (2 sticks) butter, softened**
  1 **cup packed light brown sugar**
  2 **eggs**
  2 **teaspoons vanilla**
1½ **cups cocktail peanuts, finely chopped**
    Powdered sugar (optional)

1. Preheat oven to 350°F. Combine flour, baking powder and salt in small bowl.

2. Beat butter in large bowl with electric mixer at medium speed until smooth. Gradually beat in brown sugar; increase speed to medium-high and beat until light and fluffy. Beat in eggs, one at a time, until fluffy. Beat in vanilla. Gradually stir in flour mixture until blended. Stir in peanuts.

3. Drop heaping tablespoonfuls of dough about 1 inch apart onto ungreased cookie sheets; flatten slightly.

4. Bake 12 minutes or until set. Let cookies stand on cookie sheets 5 minutes; transfer to wire racks to cool completely. Dust cookies with powdered sugar, if desired. Store in airtight container.

Makes 2½ dozen cookies

Peanut Gems

New Orleans-Style Pralines

2 cups packed light brown sugar
1 cup half-and-half
¼ teaspoon salt
2 tablespoons butter
2 tablespoons bourbon or cognac
1½ cups pecan halves

1. Line 2 baking sheets with foil. Combine brown sugar, half-and-half and salt in heavy 2- or 2½-quart saucepan. Cook over medium heat until sugar is dissolved and mixture begins to boil, stirring occasionally.

2. Attach candy thermometer to side of pan, making sure bulb is submerged in sugar mixture but not touching bottom of pan or use instant-read thermometer. Continue boiling about 20 minutes or until sugar mixture reaches soft-ball stage (235° to 240°F) on candy thermometer, stirring occasionally. (Watch carefully because candy will be grainy if overcooked.) Remove from heat; stir in butter and bourbon. Stir in pecans.

3. Beat with wooden spoon 3 to 4 minutes until temperature drops to 155°F on candy thermometer and mixture is thickened and glossy. Quickly drop pecan mixture by level measuring tablespoonfuls onto prepared baking sheets. (If mixture becomes too thick, stir in 1 to 2 teaspoons hot water and reheat over medium heat until mixture reaches 155°F on candy thermometer.) Cool completely, about 30 minutes. Store in airtight container at room temperature up to 3 days. ***Makes about 34 pralines (1¼ pounds)***

 *196*

New Orleans Style Pralines

Jolly Bourbon Balls

1 package (12 ounces) vanilla wafers, finely crushed (3 cups)
1 cup finely chopped nuts
1 cup powdered sugar, divided
1 cup (6 ounces) semisweet chocolate chips
½ cup light corn syrup
⅓ cup bourbon

1. Combine crushed wafers, nuts and ½ cup powdered sugar in large bowl; set aside.

2. Melt chocolate with corn syrup in top of double boiler over simmering (not boiling) water. Stir in bourbon until smooth. Pour chocolate mixture over crumb mixture; stir to combine thoroughly. Shape scant 1 tablespoonful of mixture into 1-inch ball. Repeat with remaining mixture. Roll balls into uniform round shapes; place on waxed paper.

3. Place remaining ½ cup powdered sugar in shallow bowl. Roll balls in powdered sugar; place in petit four or candy cases. Store in airtight containers at least 3 days before serving for flavors to mellow. (May be stored up to 2 weeks.) ***Makes about 48 candies***

With a slight taste of bourbon, these rich little confections are quick and easy to make. Substitute rum instead of bourbon and chocolate wafers instead of vanilla wafers for festive variations.

Dixie Peanut Brittle

2 cups granulated sugar
1 cup light corn syrup
½ cup water
½ teaspoon salt
3 cups raw shelled Spanish peanuts (skins on)
2 tablespoons butter
1 teaspoon vanilla extract
2 teaspoons baking soda

Heat sugar, syrup, water and salt to a rolling boil in a heavy 2-quart saucepan. Add peanuts. Reduce heat to medium and stir constantly. Cook to hard crack stage (293°F on a candy thermometer). Add butter and vanilla, then baking soda. (For safety's sake, keep in mind that the mixture will dramatically increase in volume and could spill over the sides of the saucepan.) Beat rapidly and pour onto a lightly greased baking sheet, spreading to ¼-inch thickness. When cool, break into pieces. Store in an airtight container. ***Makes about 2 pounds candy***

Favorite recipe from **Texas Peanut Producers Board**

Kentucky Bourbon Pecan Drops

1 cup (2 sticks) plus 1 tablespoon butter, softened, divided
¾ cup granulated sugar
¾ cup firmly packed light brown sugar
2 eggs
4 tablespoons bourbon, divided
2¼ cups all-purpose flour
1 teaspoon baking soda
½ teaspoon salt
1 cup coarsely chopped pecans, toasted
1 cup semisweet chocolate chips
2 tablespoons heavy cream or half-and-half
½ cup sifted powdered sugar

1. Preheat oven to 350°F. Combine 1 cup butter, granulated sugar and brown sugar in large bowl of electric mixer. Beat at medium speed until light and fluffy. Beat in eggs and 1 tablespoon bourbon. Combine flour, baking soda and salt. Gradually beat into batter at low speed until dough forms. Beat in pecans.

2. Drop heaping tablespoonfuls of dough 2 inches apart onto ungreased cookie sheets. Bake 12 to 14 minutes or until edges are golden brown. Let cookies stand on cookie sheets 1 minute. Remove to wire racks; cool completely.

3. Combine chocolate chips and remaining 1 tablespoon butter in medium microwavable bowl. Microwave at HIGH 50 seconds; stir well. If necessary, continue microwaving at 10 second intervals until chocolate is completely melted when stirred. Stir cream into chocolate. Add powdered sugar; mix well. Gradually stir in remaining 3 tablespoons bourbon; mix well. Cool completely.

4. Transfer chocolate mixture to small plastic food storage bag. Cut very tiny corner off bag. Squeeze glaze decoratively over cookies. Let stand until chocolate is set, about 20 minutes.

5. Store tightly covered at room temperature or freeze cookies up to 3 months.

Makes about 2½ dozen cookies

Kentucky Bourbon Pecan Drops

Praline Pecans & Cranberries

3½ cups pecan halves
¼ cup light corn syrup
¼ cup packed light brown sugar
2 tablespoons butter
1 teaspoon vanilla
¼ teaspoon baking soda
1½ cups dried cranberries or cherries

1. Preheat oven to 250°F. Cover large baking sheet with heavy-duty foil; set aside.

2. Grease 13×9-inch baking pan. Spread pecans in single layer in pan.

3. Combine corn syrup, brown sugar and butter in small microwavable bowl. Microwave at HIGH 1 minute; stir. Microwave 30 seconds to 1 minute or until boiling rapidly. Stir in vanilla and baking soda until well blended. Drizzle evenly over pecans; stir until evenly coated.

4. Bake 1 hour, stirring every 20 minutes with wooden spoon. Immediately transfer mixture to prepared baking sheet, spreading pecans evenly over foil with lightly greased spatula.

5. Cool completely. Break pecans apart with wooden spoon. Combine pecans and cranberries in large bowl.

6. Store in airtight container at room temperature up to 2 weeks.

Makes about 5 cups

Praline Pecans & Cranberries

FLAVORFUL
Condiments

Chunky Sweet Spiced Apple Butter

4 cups (about 1¼ pounds) peeled, chopped Granny Smith apples
¾ cup packed dark brown sugar
2 tablespoons balsamic vinegar
4 tablespoons butter, divided
1 tablespoon ground cinnamon
½ teaspoon salt
¼ teaspoon ground cloves
1½ teaspoons vanilla

SLOW COOKER DIRECTIONS

1. Combine apples, sugar, vinegar, 2 tablespoons butter, cinnamon, salt and cloves in slow cooker. Cover; cook on LOW 8 hours.

2. Stir in remaining 2 tablespoons butter and vanilla. Cool completely.

Makes 2 cups

SERVING SUGGESTIONS: Serve with roasted meats or toast.

Chunky Sweet Spiced Apple Butter

Peach Ginger Chutney

1½ cups chopped ripe DOLE® Peaches, Nectarines or Plums
⅓ cup DOLE® Orange Peach Mango Juice
¼ cup cider vinegar
¼ cup finely chopped onion
2 tablespoons packed brown sugar
1 teaspoon finely chopped crystallized ginger
   or ¼ teaspoon ground ginger
¼ teaspoon ground cinnamon
1 cup DOLE® Chopped Dates or Seedless Raisins

• Combine peaches, juice, vinegar, onion, sugar, ginger and cinnamon in medium saucepan. Bring to boil. Reduce heat to low; cook 10 minutes, stirring occasionally.

• Stir in dates; cook 10 minutes or until slightly thickened. Serve warm, at room temperature or chilled.   *Makes 16 servings*

PREP TIME: 10 minutes.
COOK TIME: 20 minutes.

To ripen peaches, nectarines, plums and bananas, try the old paper bag method: Place the fruit in a brown paper bag and keep it at room temperature. The bag traps the natural gases from the fruit and speeds up the ripening process. Just be sure to check the fruit daily, and refrigerate it as soon as it's ripe.

Pear Chutney

    1 tablespoon vegetable oil
    1 jalapeño pepper,* seeded and minced
1½ teaspoons grated fresh ginger
    1 small shallot, minced
    1 medium unpeeled ripe pear, cored and diced into ½-inch pieces
    1 tablespoon cider vinegar
    1 teaspoon brown sugar
  ⅛ teaspoon salt
    1 tablespoon water
    1 tablespoon chopped green onion

Jalapeño peppers can sting and irritate the skin; wear rubber gloves when handling peppers and do not touch eyes. Wash hands after handling.

Heat oil in medium saucepan. Add jalapeño, ginger and shallot. Cook over low heat 5 minutes or until shallot is tender. Add pear, vinegar, brown sugar and salt. Stir in 1 tablespoon water. Cover; cook over low heat 15 minutes or until pear is tender. Add 1 tablespoon water if mixture becomes dry. Stir in green onion and cook 1 minute to soften.   *Makes 2 cups*

Zesty Remoulade Sauce

    1 cup mayonnaise
    2 to 3 green onions, finely chopped
    1 rib celery, finely chopped
    2 tablespoons prepared horseradish, drained
    1 tablespoon finely chopped chives
    1 tablespoon Dijon mustard
    1 tablespoon fresh lemon juice
    1 clove garlic, finely chopped
  ½ teaspoon TABASCO® brand Pepper Sauce

Combine all ingredients in medium bowl. Cover and refrigerate 1 hour to blend flavors. Serve chilled.   *Makes 1¾ cups*

Cran-Apple Orange Conserve

2 medium oranges
5 large tart apples, peeled, cored and chopped
2 cups sugar
1½ cups fresh cranberries
1 tablespoon grated fresh lemon peel

SLOW COOKER DIRECTIONS

1. Remove a thin slice from both ends of both oranges for easier chopping. Finely chop unpeeled oranges to make 2 cups; remove any seeds. Combine oranges, apples, sugar, cranberries and lemon peel in slow cooker. Cover; cook on HIGH 4 hours. Slightly crush fruit with potato masher.

2. Cook, uncovered, on LOW 4 hours or until very thick, stirring occasionally to prevent sticking.

3. Cool at least 2 hours. *Makes about 5 cups*

SERVING SUGGESTION: Fruit conserve can be served with pound cake, roast pork or poultry.

 *208*

Cran-Apple Orange Conserve

Gingered Pineapple and Cranberries

2 cans (20 ounces each) pineapple chunks in juice, undrained
1 cup dried sweetened cranberries
½ cup brown sugar
1 teaspoon curry powder, divided
1 teaspoon grated fresh ginger, divided
¼ teaspoon red pepper flakes
2 tablespoons water
1 tablespoon cornstarch

SLOW COOKER DIRECTIONS

1. Place pineapple with juice, cranberries, brown sugar, ½ teaspoon curry powder, ½ teaspoon ginger and pepper flakes into slow cooker.

2. Cover; cook on HIGH 3 hours.

3. Combine water, cornstarch, remaining ½ teaspoon ginger and ½ teaspoon curry powder in small bowl; stir until cornstarch is dissolved. Add to pineapple mixture. Cook, uncovered, on HIGH 15 minutes or until thickened. *Makes 4½ cups*

VARIATION: Substitute 2 cans (20 ounces each) pineapple tidbits in heavy syrup for pineapple and brown sugar.

Gingered Pineapple and Cranberries

Cranberry-Apple Relish

1 package (12 ounces) fresh or frozen cranberries
1 apple, peeled and cut into eighths
½ cup packed fresh mint leaves
⅓ cup golden or dark raisins
⅓ cup packed brown sugar
⅓ cup orange marmalade
1 tablespoon lemon juice
1 tablespoon Dijon mustard

1. Combine cranberries, apple and mint in food processor; process until finely chopped.

2. Transfer cranberry mixture to medium bowl. Add raisins, brown sugar, marmalade, lemon juice and mustard; mix well. Serve with roasted poultry, pork or lamb.   *Makes 4 cups*

Spicy Cocktail Sauce

1 cup tomato ketchup
2 cloves garlic, finely chopped
1 tablespoon fresh lemon juice
1 teaspoon prepared horseradish
¾ teaspoon chili powder
½ teaspoon salt
¼ teaspoon hot pepper sauce *or* ⅛ teaspoon ground red pepper

Combine all ingredients in medium bowl; blend well. Spoon into glass bowl; serve with cooked seafood. Or, pour into clean glass jar and seal tightly. Store up to 1 month in refrigerator.

Makes 1⅓ cups sauce, enough for 1 pound of seafood

Cranberry-Apple Relish

Onion Marmalade

　1 bottle (12 ounces) balsamic vinegar
　1 bottle (12 ounces) white wine vinegar
　3 tablespoons arrowroot or cornstarch
　2 tablespoons water
1½ cups dark brown sugar
　2 teaspoons cumin seeds
　2 teaspoons coriander seeds
　4 large yellow onions, halved and thinly sliced

SLOW COOKER DIRECTIONS

1. With exhaust fan running, cook vinegars in large saucepan over high heat until reduced to ¼ cup. Sauce will be thick and syrupy. Remove from heat. Blend arrowroot and water in small cup. Add brown sugar, cumin, coriander and arrowroot mixture to sauce; blend well.

2. Place onions in slow cooker. Stir in vinegar mixture; mix well. Cover; cook on LOW 8 to 10 hours or HIGH 4 to 6 hours until onions are no longer crunchy. Stir occasionally to prevent sticking. Store in refrigerator for up to 2 weeks. *Makes 5 cups*

SERVING SUGGESTION: Serve as side dish or condiment with eggs, roasted vegetables and meats, and on sandwiches.

Quick Refrigerator Sweet Pickles

5 cups thinly sliced cucumbers
2 cloves garlic, halved
2 cups water
1 teaspoon mustard seed
1 teaspoon celery seed
1 teaspoon ground turmeric
2 cups sliced onions
1 cup julienne carrots
2 cups vinegar
1½ cups EQUAL® SPOONFUL*

*May substitute 36 packets EQUAL® sweetener.

• Place cucumbers and garlic in glass bowl. Combine water, mustard seed, celery seed and turmeric in medium saucepan. Bring to boiling.

• Add onions and carrots; cook 2 minutes. Add vinegar; bring just to boiling.

• Remove from heat; stir in Equal®. Pour over cucumbers and garlic. Cool.

• Cover and chill at least 24 hours before serving. Store in refrigerator up to 2 weeks. *Makes about 6 cups*

When the garden's produce overflows, easy-to-make sweet pickles preserve the flavor and add extra zing to relish trays and sandwiches. These quick-to-prepare crunchy refrigerator pickles will provide a cool and crunchy treat for a hot autumn day.

Refrigerator Corn Relish

2 cups cut fresh corn (4 ears) *or* **1 (10-ounce) package frozen whole-kernel corn**
½ cup vinegar
⅓ cup cold water
1 tablespoon cornstarch
¼ cup chopped onion
¼ cup chopped celery
¼ cup chopped green or red bell pepper
2 tablespoons chopped pimiento
1 teaspoon ground turmeric
½ teaspoon salt
½ teaspoon dry mustard
¼ cup EQUAL® SPOONFUL*

*May substitute 6 packets EQUAL® sweetener.

• Cook corn in boiling water until crisp-tender, 5 to 7 minutes; drain and set aside.

• Combine vinegar, water and cornstarch in large saucepan; stir until cornstarch is dissolved. Add corn, onion, celery, pepper, pimiento, turmeric, salt and mustard. Cook and stir until thickened and bubbly. Cook and stir 2 minutes more. Remove from heat; stir in Equal®. Cool. Cover and store in refrigerator up to 2 weeks.

• Serve with beef, pork or poultry.   *Makes 10 servings*

Acknowledgments

The publisher would like to thank the companies and organizations listed below for the use of their recipes and photographs in this publication.

ACH FOOD COMPANIES, INC.
Bob Evans®
Chef Paul Prudhomme's Magic Seasoning Blends®
ConAgra Foods®
Crisco is a registered trademark of The J.M. Smucker Company
Del Monte Corporation
Dole Food Company, Inc.
Domino® Foods, Inc.
Eagle Brand® Sweetened Condensed Milk
Egg Beaters®
Equal® sweetener
Filippo Berio® Olive Oil
Florida Department of Agriculture and Consumer Services, Bureau of Seafood and Aquaculture
The Golden Grain Company®
Hershey Foods Corporation
Hormel Foods, LLC
Jennie-O Turkey Store®
Kahlúa® Liqueur
The Kingsford® Products Co.
McIlhenny Company (TABASCO® brand Pepper Sauce)
National Fisheries Institute
National Honey Board
National Pork Board
Nestlé USA
Newman's Own, Inc.®
Peanut Advisory Board
Reckitt Benckiser Inc.
Sargento® Foods Inc.
Smucker's® trademark of The J.M. Smucker Company
Southeast United Dairy Industry Association, Inc.
The Sugar Association, Inc.
Reprinted with permission of Sunkist Growers, Inc.
Texas Peanut Producers Board
Unilever Foods North America

Index

Index

Index

Index

Index

Index

METRIC CONVERSION CHART

VOLUME MEASUREMENTS (dry)

1/8 teaspoon = 0.5 mL
1/4 teaspoon = 1 mL
1/2 teaspoon = 2 mL
3/4 teaspoon = 4 mL
1 teaspoon = 5 mL
1 tablespoon = 15 mL
2 tablespoons = 30 mL
1/4 cup = 60 mL
1/3 cup = 75 mL
1/2 cup = 125 mL
2/3 cup = 150 mL
3/4 cup = 175 mL
1 cup = 250 mL
2 cups = 1 pint = 500 mL
3 cups = 750 mL
4 cups = 1 quart = 1 L

VOLUME MEASUREMENTS (fluid)

1 fluid ounce (2 tablespoons) = 30 mL
4 fluid ounces (1/2 cup) = 125 mL
8 fluid ounces (1 cup) = 250 mL
12 fluid ounces (1 1/2 cups) = 375 mL
16 fluid ounces (2 cups) = 500 mL

WEIGHTS (mass)

1/2 ounce = 15 g
1 ounce = 30 g
3 ounces = 90 g
4 ounces = 120 g
8 ounces = 225 g
10 ounces = 285 g
12 ounces = 360 g
16 ounces = 1 pound = 450 g

DIMENSIONS

1/16 inch = 2 mm
1/8 inch = 3 mm
1/4 inch = 6 mm
1/2 inch = 1.5 cm
3/4 inch = 2 cm
1 inch = 2.5 cm

OVEN TEMPERATURES

250°F = 120°C
275°F = 140°C
300°F = 150°C
325°F = 160°C
350°F = 180°C
375°F = 190°C
400°F = 200°C
425°F = 220°C
450°F = 230°C

BAKING PAN SIZES

Utensil	Size in Inches/Quarts	Metric Volume	Size in Centimeters
Baking or Cake Pan (square or rectangular)	8×8×2	2 L	20×20×5
	9×9×2	2.5 L	23×23×5
	12×8×2	3 L	30×20×5
	13×9×2	3.5 L	33×23×5
Loaf Pan	8×4×3	1.5 L	20×10×7
	9×5×3	2 L	23×13×7
Round Layer Cake Pan	8×1½	1.2 L	20×4
	9×1½	1.5 L	23×4
Pie Plate	8×1¼	750 mL	20×3
	9×1¼	1 L	23×3
Baking Dish or Casserole	1 quart	1 L	—
	1½ quart	1.5 L	—
	2 quart	2 L	—